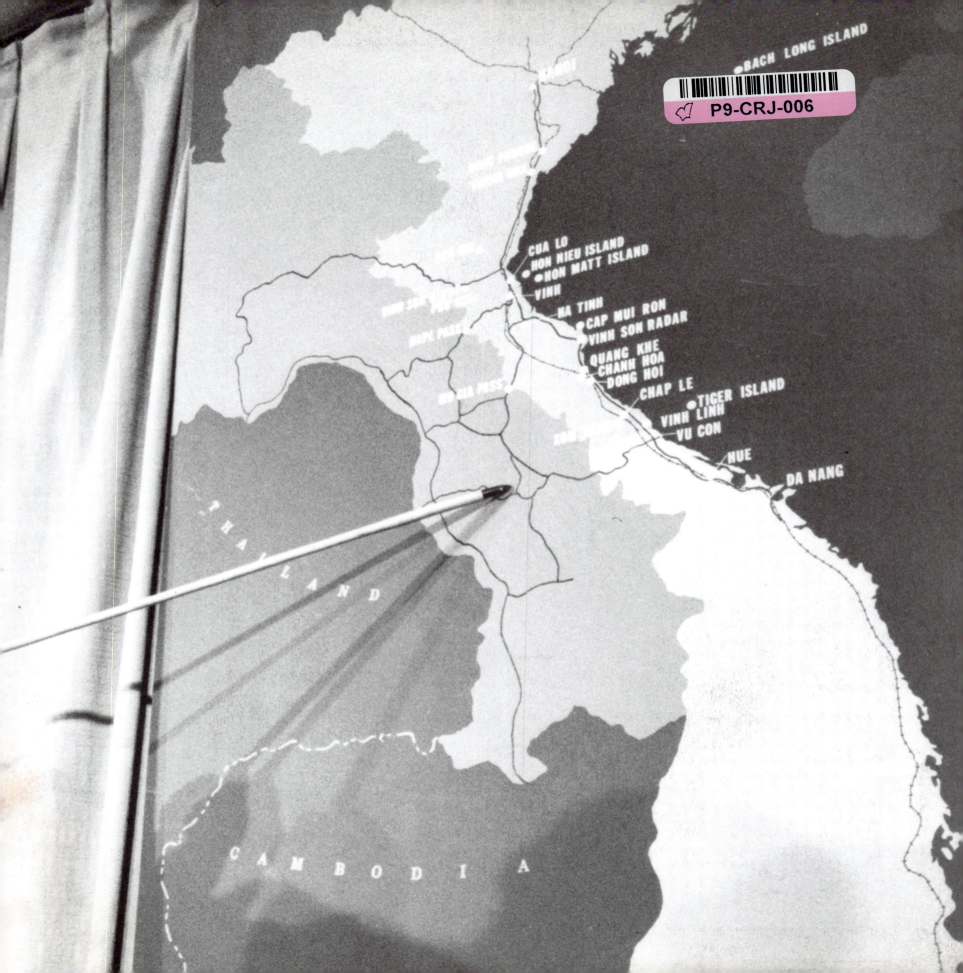

VIETNAM

A HISTORY

Written by Mike Lepine

Danann
BOOKS

CONTENTS

About the Author

Mike Lepine is a **Sunday Times No1 best-selling author.**
He has written some thirty-five books and has been
published throughout the world from America to Finland,
and from France to Japan. He has also worked extensively
in television in programming as diverse as the arts,
consumer rights and comedy. For many years the Editor of
the Aviation & Military Video Club, Mike was instrumental
with DD Home Entertainment in bringing much rare
archival film footage to the public for the very first time.

ABOVE LEFT: Illustration of the Taking of Bac Ninh, March 12 1884 | **ABOVE RIGHT:** Indochina Partisans pre-1931

207 B.C. – THE VIETNAM WAR BEGINS

'What is our history? There's nothing in our history except struggle. Struggle against foreign invaders always more powerful than ourselves...and whatever new situation arises, our people say, ah well, there it goes again...'

North Vietnamese Prime Minister Pham Van Dong.

Almost as soon as the Lac Viet people had started to build their own society, they were conquered. The Hung kings who ruled the land were swept aside by a Chinese warlord in 207 BC. He called his new conquest Nam Viet. For the next thousand years, the Vietnamese people found themselves under Chinese rule. They fought back, under charismatic leaders such as the Trung Sisters and the warrior woman Lady Trieu – but China was always too strong. It wasn't until 938 AD that a Vietnamese warlord, Ngo Quyen, managed to drive out the hated Chinese and establish the independent state of Dai Viet (Great Viet).

The Mongol hordes came – three times – and three times Dai Viet fought them off. The Chinese returned in 1407 and stayed for 20 years until the people could expel them again. The country expanded, taking in the Mekong Delta and the Central Highlands. The Chinese attempted to install a puppet ruling dynasty and were fought off once again, but their machinations split the country. Northern and southern warlords fought a brutal civil war that lasted four decades and caused a century of division. For a brief time, the country was reunified by the Tay Son brothers, before they too were swept away by the warlord Nguyen Anh at the end of the 18th Century.

Nguyen had some help from foreign friends in his rise to power. His friends were French – and they liked what they saw.

FRENCH INDOCHINA

French Catholic missionaries entered Vietnam in the 1600s. By the 1800s, their interference in the overwhelmingly Buddhist nation was causing increasing resentment at every level of Vietnamese society. The ruling dynasty knew they were conspiring against them. The peasants resented their intrusion into everyday life. Even the courtesans hated them because of their strange western morality. The growing threat to Catholic missionary work in Vietnam gave the French an excuse to act – and act harshly.

In 1858, 14 French gunboats seized Hanoi in the north. A year later, Saigon fell in the south. Now the French squeezed the Nguyen emperor for more and more territorial concessions. The pretext of protecting the missionaries was dropped. Things had moved on into out-and-out empire building. The North Vietnamese turned to their old enemies, the Chinese, for help in resisting the Western invaders. The result was a war between China and France which raged through 1884 into 1885. The Chinese lost, but Vietnamese resistance continued on for a decade led by Phan Đình Phung. In the 1890s, it's estimated that Vietnamese royalist guerrillas slaughtered fully one third of all Catholic converts in the country.

France consolidated Vietnam and Cambodia into the territory of French Indochina in 1887. They added neighbouring Laos in 1893, after provoking a war with the King of Siam. The local kings and emperors were allowed to stay on their thrones, but were rulers in name only. The French were now in charge.

HO CHI MINH

If things had turned out just a little differently, Ho Chi Minh might have passed his life peaceably as a pastry chef in Ealing.

The future leader of the resistance against French and American control of Vietnam was born Nguyen Tat Thanh in the small village of Hoang Tru in May 1890. The world he was born into was very much dominated by the French colonialists. French was the language in which anything of any importance was said or written down. The native language was fit only for peasants. Catholics ran the schools, and imparting French culture and the Christian vision of the world were seen as an important part of civilizing the natives. French architecture dominated the cities. French trade requirements shaped the economy.

Ho's father was a teacher and, as a child, Ho showed an impressive scholastic ability. At the age of ten, Ho's father renamed the boy Nguyen Tat Thanh, which meant Nguyen the Accomplished. Despite developing an early hatred of all things French, Ho dutifully attended a French university in Hue, only to lose his scholarship when his father was ejected from his government position for disciplining a corrupt local official.

With no hope of being able to afford an education, Ho went to sea, working his passage in the kitchen of a French steamer. He pitched up first in France in 1911 before working his way to America. From 1912-3 he lived in New York City and Boston, working as everything from a baker in hotel kitchens to a line manager on General Motors' automobile assembly line. From 1913-1919, Ho lived in Britain, and gave serious consideration to developing a career as a pastry chef while he lived in Ealing, West London.

1919 found him in France teaming up with other footloose socialists and radicals. The powers that had just won the First World War were busy hammering out the terms of the Treaty of Versailles. Ho and his compatriots lobbied them passionately for increased freedom for the people of Vietnam in the post-war brave new world – but no one was particularly interested in the issue – or in them. While he was there, Ho also helped to found the French communist party – but found few within its ranks particularly interested in his nationalist cause.

Ho now moved on to Soviet Russia before turning up in China, where he preached communism, got married and sold a rival communist revolutionary out to the French secret service in Shang-Hai. When anti-communist feelings in China got too hot Ho started globetrotting again, living everywhere from India to Italy – but never daring to set foot back in Vietnam. Now he developed TB, was widely suspected of being a government agent and was reported dead by British authorities in Hong Kong as a way of avoiding a diplomatic row with the French. He was a busy man.

By 1940, the former Nguyen Tat Thanh had taken to calling himself Ho Chi Minh – which crudely translates means something like The Enlightened Spirit Mr. Smith.

ABOVE: Various images of Ho Chi Minh thoughout his life | **LEFT IMAGE:** With God daughter Élisabeth and her Mother (Lucie Aubrac)

THE SECOND WORLD WAR

Conquerors are themselves sometimes conquered. All it takes is someone bigger, more ambitious and more vicious than they are. In 1940, France fell to the armies of Nazi Germany. Out in French Indochina, the Japanese pounced. Nominally, Vietnam remained in the hands of the Vichy French administration, which was under the ultimate control of the Germans. However, the Japanese reached agreement with the Vichy government to move into Vietnam and use it as a base of operations. It was a tense and fragile arrangement, often breached. The French hated the Japanese. The Japanese despised the French. And the Vietnamese loathed them both.

The Japanese were strutting about, promising 'Asia for Asians' – but the Vietnamese were under no illusion about who was now in charge. Despite proclaiming themselves as 'liberators' of the Vietnamese people, they now began to impose their own culture just as the French had done before. Vietnamese people were encouraged to learn Japanese. The country was flooded with symbols of Japanese culture. The Japanese even tried their own 'Hearts & Minds' campaign, as the Americans would twenty years later. No one was fooled. The Vietnamese had heard about the atrocities perpetrated against their neighbours the Chinese by their Japanese conquerors and knew their true nature. One unnamed peasant is quoted as saying:

'The Japanese are a hundred times crueller than the French. Even a worm or a cricket could not live under their brutal violence'.

In exile in China, Ho Chi Minh saw his chance. He moved back into Vietnam and started fermenting trouble against both the French and the newly arrived Japanese. Perhaps to his surprise, he quickly found that his ideas were popular not just amongst the peasants but also with the more sophisticated urban population. A truly representative resistance movement was born – the Viet Minh - combining communism with nationalism. There was something for everyone.

While the Viet Minh's influence started to spread southward out of their bases on the Chinese border, Ho found himself a prisoner of Chinese nationalist forces – and then he was freed by a strange set of circumstances.

The American O.S.S. – the forerunner of the C.I.A. – were looking for an ally to work for them in bringing the fight to the Japanese forces in Vietnam as part of the greater war being waged in the East. Although officially an enemy, they were in informal talks with the Chinese guerrilla leader Mao-Tse-Tung behind the Chinese Nationalists' backs. Mao recommended Ho – who was then masquerading as Mr. C. M. Hoo. Without mentioning Mao, the O.S.S. arranged for Ho's release from Chinese custody and he became America's man in Vietnam. Now the O.S.S. began arming the Viet Minh against the Japanese and training their men in guerrilla warfare. In a single month, it's estimated that American agents trained over 200 men who would one day form the hard core leadership of North Vietnam. The very men the Americans would one day fight. Among them was Vo Nguyen Giap, a former history teacher who would go on to become North Vietnam's most outstanding military leader. His men called him Nui Lua – the 'ice-covered volcano'.

Alongside the Americans and with their full support, the Viet Minh waged a fierce guerrilla war against the Japanese inside Vietnam until the atomic strikes on Hiroshima and Nagasaki brought the Second World War to a close.

INSET: 1940. 2000 Japanese arriving at Haiphong Port, Tonkin, Indochina
RIGHT: Japanese troops entering Saigon on September 15, 1941

HAIPHONG

POST WAR VIETNAM

As Imperial Japan collapsed in abject surrender, Ho realised that his moment had come. It was now or never.

The Viet Minh occupied the northern city of Hanoi and declared a provisional government. On the same day as Japan signed formal papers of surrender out in Tokyo Bay – September 2nd 1945 – Ho stood up and declared that Vietnam was now at last an independent nation – with himself as president. With one eye on gaining U.S. support for his ambitions, he made a point of quoting from the American Declaration of Independence.

'We hold the truth that all men are created equal, that they are endowed by their Creator with certain unalienable rights, among them life, liberty and the pursuit of happiness. This immortal statement is extracted from the Declaration of Independence of the United States of America in 1776. These are undeniable truths.'

The silence from President Truman was deafening. It was obvious he couldn't care less. Ho wrote a flurry of letters to Truman looking for American support.

They were ignored.

Ho was hurt and confused by the complete lack of support from his American allies. As he had told his O.S.S. contact, the Vietnamese loved America and admired its history. Like the Vietnamese, the Americans had once fought for their liberty against a foreign empire. *'All we want is America's moral support,'* he pleaded. The problem of course was that Ho was a communist and that was first and foremost what America saw. The field agents who

worked with Ho agreed almost to a man that Ho was above all a nationalist. He believed that communism was the best way forward for an agrarian nation like Vietnam, but he was far more interested in Vietnamese national identity. Ho even gave thought to abandoning his communist beliefs and instead adopting 'Republican Nationalism'. Had America understood this, and worked with Ho, there would very likely have never been a Vietnam War.

Without American support, Ho's brief regime was doomed. Ho might have had some control over areas of the North, but events would rapidly spin way out of his control. An army of 150,000 Chinese nationalists descended on Hanoi in September 1945 and looted the city. On September 13th, British forces arrived in the southern city of Saigon to help the French regain control of their empire and released 1,400 French soldiers from Japanese internment camps. The ex-P.O.W.'s teamed up with the French civilian population of Saigon and went on a bloody mission of revenge, slaughtering any Viet Minh sympathisers they could find – and their families. Two days later, a notorious Vietnamese criminal gang in Saigon retaliated by murdering 150 European civilians including women and children.

The writing was on the wall. O.S.S. Agent Lt. Col. A. Peter Dewey filed a confidential report back to his bosses in Washington strongly recommending that America *'ought to clear out of South East Asia'*. On September 4th 1945, he was murdered by Viet Minh guerrillas, who mistook him for a French soldier. Colonel Dewey was the first American serviceman to be killed in Vietnam. Ho was horrified. He offered to write a personal letter of apology to the American President and swore that no American would ever die in Vietnam again, except over his dead body.

A month later, General Jacques Philippe Leclerc led a force of 35,000 French soldiers into South Vietnam to retake the country and drive the Viet Minh out of Saigon. Their response was to initiate a guerrilla war against the French.

ABOVE: General Philippe Leclerc and Ho Chi Minh, during negotiations for Vietnamese independence, March 1946
ABOVE RIGHT: General Leclerc Presiding Over The Departure Of Chinese Troops From Indochina 1946 **LEFT:** Harry S Truman

By the end of the year, the country was effectively split between a French dominated South and a communist controlled North.

1946

As Vietnam teetered on the brink of anarchy, Ho visited France to plead for independence for a reunited Vietnam. The French refused to make any concessions. They wanted their colonies back – and Indochina was perhaps the jewel in the crown of their empire. To emphasise their point, the French declared that South Vietnam was to be regarded as a separate nation in its own right from now on.

Ho decided to fight. His Viet Minh stepped up the volume and ferocity of their attacks on colonial forces in the autumn of 1946. The French response in turn was to bomb Haiphong Harbour and seize the northern capital of Hanoi in December 1946 with overwhelming force. Ho and what was left of his Viet Minh took refuge in the jungle to reorganise, pursued by French paratroopers. France's response was typically defiant.

French military commander General Jean-Etienne Valluy simply stated: *'If these (people) want a fight, they'll get it.'*

The First Indochina War had begun. It would last for eight years.

THE FIRST INDOCHINA WAR

Driven into hiding, the Viet Minh under General Giap spent the first few years of the war dodging any major military encounters with French forces as best they could. During 1947, the French went after them in a big way and, during Operation Lea, managed to kill up to 9,000 guerrillas. The French also reinstated the deposed Vietnamese emperor, Bao Dai, and started to build what they hoped would be a more effective Vietnamese Army to defend against insurgency.

In 1949, Mao-Tse-Tung seized control of China and prioritised support for the communist guerrillas in Vietnam. Suddenly almost spoiled for supplies, General Giap began to organise his forces into a regular army comprising some five full divisions. The Viet Minh were now in a position to go on the attack. Their first targets were French military outposts along the Chinese border. In February 1950, they overran the small French Garrison at Lai Khe in Tonkin. Bases at Cao Bang and Đong Khe fell the same year. The biggest disaster for the French in 1950 though was undoubtedly the loss of Lang Son, which was manned by a force of 4,000 elite French Foreign Legionnaires. There was chaos as the bases started to fall. Retreating French troops were constantly ambushed and relief columns subjected to relentless attacks as they fought their way to help. Elite paratroopers dropped in to the combat zone found themselves trapped, overwhelmed and almost annihilated. Of an original force of some 10,000 men, almost five thousand were killed or captured. Another two thousand were wounded. In Hanoi, there was talk of

French Troops In Action During The Tonkin Campaign In December 1946

evacuating the city.

That same year, America decided to take a fateful stance on Vietnam. Alarmed by Mao's takeover of China, the U.S.A. started to help fund the French war against the Viet Minh. They now saw Ho's nationalist movement as nothing more than a tool of Chinese expansionism – and they would continue to hold this view for decades – unaware of the Viet people's historical mistrust and even hatred of the Chinese, based on their long history of conquest. America's contribution to the war effort was small at first – just $10 million - but by just 1954 the U.S. contribution to the French war effort would top $1,000 million. America also sent its first military advisors into the country to accompany the money. They were not welcomed by the French. Nevertheless, America was now both involved and committed. When then Vice President Nixon came to Hanoi in 1953, he made a strong statement of intent to support the French, saying *'It is impossible to lay down arms until victory is won.'*

The Americans had little impact at first. It was the decision by the new French commander, General Jean Marie de Lattre de Tassigny, to build a fortified line from Hanoi across to Tonkin to contain the Viet Minh forces that changed the fortunes of the war. The tactic worked. In January 1951, the Viet Minh suffered their first solid military defeat, as Giap sent his forces against the garrison at Vĩnh Yen, which was part of what became known as the de Lattre Line, just North West of Hanoi. 6,000 French Foreign Legionnaires were waiting for them. The attacking Viet Minh found themselves exposed in open ground – and the Legionnaires had set up 'kill zones'. As the attack progressed, Giap's troops were raked by wave after wave of lethally effective machine gun fire and bombarded by highly accurate French artillery barrages. In just three days, the Viet Minh lost 6,000 men and saw 500 more captured and 8,000 wounded.

Giap tried his luck again, striking simultaneously at Phu Ly, Ninh Bình, and Phat Diem. All three assaults were repulsed with considerable loss of life on the communist side. French commanders then launched a powerful counterattack, killing another 10,000 of Giap's men as they tried to find sanctuary in the jungle. The losses sustained shook the Viet Minh high command – and the de Lattre line seemed impregnable. At the end of 1951, the French came out from behind the de Lattre Line and dropped paratroopers on the enemy-held territory around Hoa Binh. They managed to hold the territory for just three months before the Viet Minh drove them back to the de Lattre Line again. It proved that, despite the heavy losses they had sustained, the Viet Minh were still a formidable force to be reckoned with in their own areas, and both sides lost around 5,000 men during the fighting.

In October 1952, the French decided to rely on what they called 'Hedgehog' tactics, establishing large, well-fortified bases to tempt out the Viet Minh and get them to engage in conventional rather than guerrilla warfare. In 1953, the new French commander in Indochina, General Henri Navarre, pioneered the 'Search and Destroy' tactics which the Americans would adopt a decade later. However, Navarre was never convinced that the war in Indochina was winnable and – as rumours of peace talks started up, he looked at achieving a way that France could bargain from a position of maximum strength and then make an 'exit with honour'.

DIEN BIEN PHU

We will take the French by the throat'
General Giap

Dien Bien Phu was a Vietnamese town and the site of an abandoned WWII Japanese airbase some 200 miles behind Viet Minh lines. By stationing a large, well-armed and well prepared French force here, Navarre thought he could not only severely restrict Viet Minh raids into Laos but also tempt Giap into a large scale stand up, conventional fight. A fight that might shatter and destroy the Viet Minh once and for all.

The plan was similar to that which the French had used at Na San in 1952, where communist forces had dashed themselves almost to destruction upon the garrison's defences. Giap too had noticed the similarity – but this time he was prepared to adopt very different tactics. The terrain at Dien Bien Phu was different. The French here were essentially at the bottom of a very large valley, where they could be encircled and attacked from the densely wooded hillsides above. Thanks to the Chinese, Giap now had access to far better weapons than he had at Na San. He now had heavy artillery – his 'steel elephants' - which were dragged to the battlefield on ropes by teams of peasants half an inch at a time and then hidden in burrowed out caves and tunnels around the French base. Dien Bien Phu was also at the very limit of French capabilities to supply by air – and the Chinese had given Giap a generous supply of anti-aircraft guns too.

French troops began to arrive in November 1953. Within weeks, six battalions of elite paratroopers were stationed there. They were supported by heavy artillery and ten M24 Chaffee light tanks. They arranged the defences around seven strongholds, with a central command post between them. What they didn't know that there were now 50,000 Viet Minh guerrillas gathering in the hills above. When they started to have an inkling of just how great the Viet Minh force was, reinforcements were raced into place – but not nearly enough.

The Viet Minh attack began with determined ambushes on French patrols whenever they left the safety of the base to range the surrounding hills. Many were wiped out. Then on March 13th 1954, Giap's big guns began to

ABOVE LEFT: French Paras go into action at Dien Bien Phu | **ABOVE CENTRE:** Col. Christian de Castries, French commander at Dien Bien Phu
ABOVE RIGHT: French M24 Chaffee tank in action in Vietnam **OPPOSITE PAGE:** 1946: IndoChina war. French soldier discovers Vietnamese corpse

open up on the base itself. The French artillery tried to respond but couldn't spot their targets. In shame, the French artillery commander apologised to his brother officers and then killed himself with a grenade. Viet Minh troops raced in after the bombardment. One of the seven French strongholds was hit by wave after wave of Viet Minh suicide squads (Giap called them his 'death-braving volunteers') and fell in just hours. Counter-attacks to retake it failed. A second stronghold fell shortly after. Yet another fell when local troops thought loyal to the French simply turned tail and fled. A determined artillery blitz put the airfield out of commission too. All further supply would have be dropped in haphazardly by parachute. The French had now lost a number of key strongholds, their airfield had been destroyed and they realised that they were completely trapped.

The events at Dien Bien Phu shook the Western world. The French were suddenly in desperate trouble and the Western powers recognised it. Events are still shrouded in secrecy, but it's rumoured that U.S. Secretary of State John Foster Dulles offered French Foreign Minister Georges Bidault two atomic bombs to 'sort things out'. The French declined. They knew that resorting to tactical nuclear weapons in the field would most likely wipe out their own men. The Americans also considered 'going in' with troops to assist the French, but Congress would only agree if the British went with them – and then British Prime Minister Winston Churchill was having none of it. Among the fiercest Congressional critics of American involvement were future presidents John F. Kennedy and Lyndon B. Johnson. The French were on their own.

Back at Dien Bien Phu, none of this was known. The besieged French hunkered down and waited for the American cavalry to arrive and save the day. They would never come. Planning in the hills above, Giap tried to capitalise on his early success with more mass waves of fanatical suicide troops descending on the base, but these were torn to pieces by coordinated action from French warplanes and base artillery. Now, it was the turn of the Viet Minh to be shocked, and French radio operators inside Dien Bien Phu picked up angry radio exchanges from the hills above as guerrilla units started to mutiny rather than launch fresh assaults.

Faced with widespread dissent in his ranks, Giap switched tactics. He stopped the mass suicide attacks temporarily and took a slower, more cautious approach. He brought in Katusha rockets, increased the bombardment and had constructed a one hundred mile network of six foot deep trenches to allow his troops to advance in more safety. By April 22nd, the Viet Minh had overrun the airfield bringing an end to resupply by parachute for the base. Then on May 1st, Giap switched tactics again. He unleashed a massive wave of troops against the base, overrunning more of the surviving strongholds. Furious mass assaults then followed on the 6th and 7th. At 5pm on the 7th, French commanders back in Hanoi received a last desperate message from Dien Bien Phu.

'The Viets are everywhere. The situation is very grave. I feel the end is approaching but we will fight to the finish.'

By nightfall on May 7th, it was all over. Dien Bien Phu was in communist hands at the cost of some 8,000 Viet Minh lives. The Viet Minh took almost 11,000 French soldiers prisoner. Less than four thousand would survive their ordeal in captivity. A larger number of Indochinese soldiers loyal to the French were also captured. None were ever seen alive again.

French troops take cover in their trenches while being shelled from the hazy hills in the distance

AFTER THE FALL

The war in Indochina had never been popular with French public opinion, as is often the case with faraway foreign wars. The country was still struggling to recover from the horror, damage and trauma of the Second World War. Furthermore, intellectuals and hard line communists were agitating furiously against the war at every opportunity. In response, French authorities had tried to use colonial soldiers and foreign mercenaries in the fight wherever possible. In that way, fewer bodies would come back to the cities, towns and villages of France. Instead they would come back to the cities, towns and villages of Algeria, Morocco and other colonies.

For the French, the fall of Dien Bien Phu was the last straw. They knew now that they had lost the war against the Viet Minh and that it was time to withdraw. The international community would be charged with cleaning up the mess they had left behind. Over 75,000 French and Colonial troops had died in the war and veterans returning home would find themselves treated with contempt by the civilian population.

America would now step up to support Vietnam in France's place. They saw no choice. Vietnam didn't matter of itself. It was nothing. It was nowhere. No one could even find it on a map. But if Vietnam fell to the communists, American politicians reasoned, then other - more important - east Asian countries might be brought tumbling down too. They called this 'The Domino Theory'.

THE DOMINO THEORY

After the Second World War, one of America's strongest foreign policy aims was to bring about the end of the old European empires - despite their status as allies. This was not born of a sudden concern for the inalienable rights of native peoples in far-flung lands. This was no rediscovery of the spirit of 1776. Empires acted as restrictive trade practices. America wanted to open up vast new commercial markets in the newly-freed territories and feed their own industries.

Almost at once, the idea went wrong. What America had not anticipated was the birth of ravenous and ruthless new empires ready to fill the political vacuum left by the departing Europeans. The Soviet Union seized much of Eastern Europe, while Communist China looked South for conquest. Between 1950 and 1953, the Korean War had seen U.S. forces pitted directly against the Red Chinese army. Over 35,000 American troops had died fighting, nuclear weapons were very nearly brought into play and the outcome had been a very messy and unsatisfactory stalemate. In Malaya, the British were bearing the brunt of an 'emergency' fought by communist ethnic Chinese that would drag on from 1948 to 1960. A new reality began to dawn on the Americans. They were not going to get their fine new world full of free markets. Quite to the contrary. If they didn't do something, communism was going to sweep the pot.

The 'Domino Theory' began to enter into American strategic thinking. If one country in Asia was allowed to fall to the communists, the surrender of that country would directly endanger those surrounding it. Soon, those too would fall.

Although he didn't directly use the phrase 'Domino Theory', American President Dwight D. Eisenhower first introduced the concept to a wider world during a press

French troops leaving as Viet Minh troops enter the city

ABOVE LEFT: Ngo Dinh Diem with 3 lieutenant generals Nguyen Van Xuan, Nguyen Van Hinh and Le Van Vien in the Independence Palace, Saigon in 1954
ABOVE RIGHT: Viet Cong Soldiers

conference on the emergency in Indochina on April 7th 1954. As Dien Bien Phu teetered on the brink of being overrun, he told reporters:

'Finally, you have broader considerations that might follow what you would call the "falling domino" principle. You have a row of dominoes set up, you knock over the first one, and what will happen to the last one is the certainty that it will go over very quickly. So you could have a beginning of a disintegration that would have the most profound influences.'

No matter what it truly wanted, America had realised that it was the only force capable of protecting south-east Asia from falling into the hands of the communists. It would have to get more heavily involved.

DIVISION

Within days of the fall of Dien Bien Phu, the international powers meeting in Geneva were determining the fate of French Indochina. Representatives had gathered from America, China, France and Vietnam.

It was quickly decided that a general ceasefire would come into effect and that Vietnam would be divided – temporarily - along the 17th Parallel. Between them would lie a buffer or 'DeMilitarized Zone', which soon became referred to as the DMZ. The South would remain 'free' and Ho Chi Minh's Viet Minh would take charge of the North. The eventual fate of the country as a whole would be decided by joint democratic elections set for 1956. Laos and Cambodia were to be neutral and autonomous.

As the borders went up, people were given 300 days to move freely between North and South. Around one million streamed South, often Catholics in fear of persecution by the communist regime now in Hanoi. By

contrast only 150,000 headed north.

As the defeated French retired from their former colony, the Americans fatefully stepped in to fill the vacuum. They swiftly deposed the unpopular Vietnamese emperor and replaced him with the equally unpopular Ngo Dinh Diem as President of a notionally democratic South Vietnam.

DIEM

Born in 1901, Ngo Dinh Diem was a dapper little man fond of fine French tailoring and chain smoking whose feet usually couldn't reach the floor when he sat on a chair. He was a staunch anti-communist who was more than happy to work with the Americans – just as he had been more than happy to work with the French and the Japanese before him. Diem claimed to have been descended from a powerful Mandarin family, but this is most likely untrue and he was really of lowly birth. He was Catholic and despised Buddhists, who made up the vast bulk of the country. He was also massively corrupt, and won his 1955 elections when over 350,000 more people than there were voters in the country gave him the thumbs up. There were widespread reports of those who refused to vote for him being beaten up.

Diem was a recluse who rarely left his splendid palace. He was paranoid. He was ruthless. He was murderous. He employed his youngest brother Nhu to run the new secret police, oversee death squads and recruit torturers. In private, good brother Nhu was a heroin addict and a Nazi fantasist. Unmarried since his wife had fled into a nunnery, Diem installed his vicious and wildly fascistic sister-in-law – Madame Nhu - as First Lady and she toured the world spouting venom and creating diplomatic havoc. For the Americans, Diem

ABOVE LEFT: Captured communist photo shows VC crossing a river | **ABOVE CENTRE:** A Viet Cong soldier crouches in a bunker with an SKS rifle
ABOVE RIGHT: A Marine leads a Viet Cong suspect during a search and clear operation

was trouble waiting to happen. But he was the best they could get.

THE BIRTH OF THE VIET CONG

They called themselves the National Liberation Front for South Vietnam or The Liberation Army of South Vietnam. It was the South Vietnamese who called the guerrilla army growing within their borders the Viet Cong (Literally : Communist Vietnamese).

When Vietnam had been partitioned in 1954, Hanoi specifically instructed around 10,000 loyal Viet Minh guerrillas to remain behind in the South. Their job was to secretly promote communism and to agitate against the Western-backed South Vietnamese regime. They would also sometimes pretend to be Buddhist groups to stir up religious hatred. They maintained a very low level insurgency at first. Their masters in Hanoi were desperate to use them to more aggressive ends but neither their Chinese nor Russian backers thought the time was right.

Things started to change when, in 1957, the Viet Cong launched what it called the 'extermination of traitors' campaign. Guerrillas attacked bars with machine guns, assassinated a district chief and his family and planted bombs in Saigon which left 13 Americans wounded.

By 1959, The North was ready to wage what it called a 'people's war' against the South and began pumping men and supplies down the Ho Chi Minh Trail. In July 1959, the Viet Cong succeeded in killing two American military advisors at Bien Hoa. Two months later, squads of Viet Cong inflicted heavy losses on two companies of A.R.V.N. (the South Vietnamese Army) troops caught in a lethal ambush. More importantly, it was fast taking over control of the South

Vietnamese countryside and its 12,000 villages, killing village leaders who opposed it, terrorising the people into submission with torture and gang rape, taxing the peasants and teaching communist ideology to a literally captive audience.

As Viet Cong attacks escalated, the North sought to pretend that they had nothing to do with events and that the Viet Cong were an expression of a spontaneous uprising by the heroic peasant workers of South Vietnam. Of course, this was a complete pack of lies. Hanoi controlled everything. In January 1960, there were 180 Viet Cong attacks. By September that year, that figure had risen to 545. Between 1961 and 1963, approximately 40,000 troops were sent along the Ho Chi Minh Trail to join the guerrilla units fighting in the south.

Badge of Ho Chi Minh People's Revolutionary Youth Union

THE HO CHI MINH TRAIL

Essential to Northern infiltration of South Vietnam was the Ho Chi Minh Trail. It was, according to an N.S.A. analysis, nothing less than *'one of the great achievements of military engineering of the 20th century'.*

The Ho Chi Minh Trail was a pathway (in fact, many thousands of interlocking pathways) that stretched almost 1,000 kilometres from North Vietnam through Laos and Cambodia and into South Vietnam, with a spider web of alternate routes and paths comprising in total, 16,000 traversable kilometers. It passed through some of the most daunting terrain on earth, over mountains, across rivers and through thick jungle and primeval rainforests. Parts of it were ancient and had been carved out millennia ago by smugglers and bandits. Other parts had been added only during the recent First Indochina War to facilitate the movement of Viet Minh guerrilla forces.

It was the Americans who called it the Ho Chi Minh Trail. To the North Vietnamese it was The Truong Son Trail. In 1959, as part of expanding their guerrilla war against the south, the North Vietnamese began to enlarge and improve the trail. It was estimated that some 40,000 workers were required just to keep it open. They built bridges and later roads suitable for trucks to use. They hacked out giant 'rest stops' where large units of infiltrators could rest and camp, and excavated underground command centres. They established secret arms caches and fuel dumps and built false trail branches to nowhere to confuse enemy patrols.

At first, only a few supplies were funnelled down the trail. By December 1959, Viet Cong guerrillas in the South had been supplied with a total of 1,667 infantry weapons, 788 machetes and swords, 188 kg of explosives and some other miscellaneous materials.

A journey down the trail in 1959 could take a guerrilla as long as six months to complete. Later in the war, the trail had been engineered to such a fine degree that traversing it could be achieved in just six weeks. It's estimated that at least 10% of all

ABOVE: Villagers and soldiers on the Ho Chi Minh Trail | **RIGHT:** Viet Cong Guerillas assemble shells and rockets delivered along the Ho Chi Minh Trail

guerrillas died while using the route, most usually from contracting diseases such as malaria, although snake bite was an ever-common danger.

The South Vietnamese and their American allies knew perfectly well what was happening, but blocking the trail proved an almost impossible task. Much of it passed through neutral Laos and Cambodia into which they could not trespass – and almost all of it was hidden from aerial reconnaissance by the thick jungle canopy. The Americans tried using defoliants – most notably the highly toxic Agent Orange - to clear the jungle canopy – but the task was ultimately just too daunting.

In the years ahead, the Americans would try carpet bombings from Giant B-52 bombers cruising six miles high. At the height of the war, 900 bombing sorties a day were being flown against the trail – but it was reckoned that it took three full bomb loads just to kill one communist – despite each B-52 bomber being able to flatten an area one mile long and a quarter of a mile wide. They tried pioneering electronic sensors to help find the guerrillas – including innovative ones that could 'smell' human sweat – but the communists soon discovered that human sweat smells just like buffalo urine. They would hang up bags of urine in deserted areas close to the censors and watch as the Americans wasted millions of dollars bombing the wrong target. Even the C.I.A. would get involved. Having discovered that the North Vietnamese were partial to the odd bottle of Budweiser (or two, or three), they planned to 'Bud-Bomb' the enemy and retard their progress by forcing them into drunken stupors. Unfortunately the bottles kept breaking in parachute tests. The C.I.A. even tried to train pigeons with bombs strapped to them to be attracted to trucks but again with no luck.

The Ho Chi Minh Trail would become one of the defining strategic factors of The Vietnam War.

SOUTH VIETNAM 1954-1959

Ngo Dinh Diem was not a very good president. Crucially, as the Americans were very quick to learn, he was not even a very good puppet president. Not for the first time in history – and certainly not for the last – America had backed a little idiot.

Almost as soon as he came into power, Diem cancelled the reunifying elections agreed at Geneva in 1954. America was secretly ok with his decision as everyone believed that the communists would sweep any free and fair election in both the north and south. South Vietnam held its own elections in 1959 – but as many anti-government candidates were denounced as Viet Cong and therefore faced the death penalty – opposition was at best severely muted.

It was left to Diem's drug-addled brother Nhu to reinvigorate the Army of the Republic of Vietnam (A.R.V.N.) and to indulge his own Nazi-fuelled fantasies with his private anti-communist death squads. It's rumoured that, in four years when Nhu's anti-communist activities were at their height, more Vietnamese died than in all the post-war conflicts with the French.

NORTH VIETNAM 1954-1963

In the North, things were little better. There were no elections, rigged or otherwise. Ho was President and would be for life. The communists had initiated a programme of 'land reforms', something which started out as a way of giving land to the peasants and ended up – as communist land reforms tend to do – with anything up to 500,000 innocent people lying dead for reasons no-one could quite grasp. Contemporary reports record that people were

shot, buried alive, crushed under stones, beheaded, or rather prosaically just beaten to death. Very often, their entire families would die too, usually from starvation as they were denounced as enemies of the state and others were forbidden to help them. In Ho Chi Minh's own province, 6,000 peasants died rising up against communist land reforms. Still more died in famines as the land reforms wrecked the harvests.

From Hanoi, North Vietnam was ruled with an iron fist by the Vietnamese Workers Party. No dissent was tolerated. Private property was criminalised and anyone speaking out swiftly thrown into forced labour camps. Intellectuals were singled out and hunted down, their works destroyed. If they were lucky enough to be spared the firing squad, they would be brutalised in camps. People were encouraged – by bullet and bayonet if necessary – to revere Ho Chi Minh. Ho now had his own personality cult, just as Mao did in neighbouring China.

THE KENNEDY YEARS

'In the final analysis, it is their war. They are the ones who have to win it or lose it. We can help them, we can give them equipment, we can send our men out there as advisers, but they have to win it, the people of Vietnam, against the Communists.'

President John F. Kennedy, 1963.

John F. Kennedy was inaugurated as the President of the United States on January 20th 1961. As his new administration prepared to take over the White House, outgoing President Eisenhower took Kennedy aside and gave him a frank warning. He said, *'I think you're going to have to send troops to Vietnam'*.

This was something Kennedy would hear time and time again from his military and civilian advisors. It was something he would always fight to resist. Kennedy had come into office when the Cold War was at its hottest. He would face crisis after crisis and – compared with nuclear missiles in Cuba just 90 miles off the coast of Florida – Vietnam was very far away. It was one more problem he didn't need.

Kennedy's instincts were to keep the Vietnamese conflict as small as possible, to keep backing the South Vietnamese regime under President Diem and to feed them money and arms instead of American boys. In 1961, this amounted to a cost of around $1 million a day to the American economy. Despite Kennedy's best intentions, the number of American personnel in Vietnam during his presidency would rise from 900 to 16,000. French President Charles de Gaulle told him bluntly:

'I predict to you that you will – step by step – be sucked into a bottomless military and political quagmire'.

In May 1961 Kennedy's Vice President, Lyndon B. Johnson, went on a fact-finding mission to South Vietnam. He came back publicly proclaiming President Diem as *'The Winston Churchill of Asia'*. In private he was less enthusiastic but conceded that Diem was *'the only boy we have'*. That same month Kennedy sent 400 Green Berets to Vietnam to train A.R.V.N. forces in counter-insurgency warfare and to establish CIDGs (Civilian Irregular Defence Groups). These CIDGs would comprise ferocious Montagnard tribespeople to help block N.V.A. troops infiltrating into the South through their mountain territory.

By the autumn of 1961, Viet Cong attacks were becoming ever more numerous and deadly. They effectively controlled much of the countryside outside the cities. Kennedy

President John F. Kennedy

was reminded by his advisors of the Domino Theory and urged to do much more to support the South. In October, two of his top aides begged him to send more special advisors as well as 8,000 combat troops. His Defence Secretary Robert McNamara wanted to go much further. Backed by the Joint Chiefs of Staff, he strongly advised Kennedy to send 200,000 combat troops – six full divisions – into Vietnam. The communists, McNamara said bluntly, respected nothing but force.

Kennedy refused the combat troops. He did however send more military advisors together with helicopter units comprising some 300 aircraft to lift A.R.V.N. troops into battle. These Americans could now direct A.R.V.N. forces in combat and were themselves effectively going into battle (although Kennedy was quick to always deny this).

In March 1962, Operation Sunrise saw the start of the Strategic Hamlets programme, where peasants from tiny villages were forced into larger settlements which could – it was thought – be more easily defended against the Viet Cong. The ordinary people hated it – and it proved useless in any tactical sense. Over 50 of these new 'Hamlets' were very quickly taken over by the Viet Cong. Diem's response was swift and brutal. Hamlets lost to the enemy were blitzed by the South Vietnamese Air Force. American pilots unofficially also took part in the raids. Civilian casualties were high. The Strategic Hamlets policy turned many ordinary Vietnamese people against Diem's regime and made them more sympathetic to the communists. They also began to hate the Americans more, as they were seen as partners in the programme. None of this registered with the American administration at the time though. After Defence Secretary McNamara returned from a visit to South Vietnam he proudly declared, *'we are winning the war!'*

Apart from forcibly relocating large chunks of the peasantry, President Diem was making himself progressively unpopular in other ways too. Diem hated communists as much as he loved God. Diem was a Catholic in a country where 90% of people were Buddhists. Despite this, he favoured Catholics in every aspect of life. Catholics got the jobs in government and administration. Only Catholics got to be officers in the A.V.R.N. In the defended hamlets, only Catholics were trusted with weapons. Out in the countryside, no-one did anything when Catholic priests started running their own private militias who converted 'heathen Buddhists' to Catholicism at gunpoint. Majority Catholic villages got grants. Catholic Universities were well funded and the Church remained the largest single landowner in the country. Can Lao, the President's own political party, was only open to Catholics. In 1959, Diem had outraged his people when he devoted South Vietnam to the Virgin Mary and instructed that the flag of the Vatican would be flown over many state buildings.

By 1963, the bulk of the Buddhist population in the South had had enough. There were mass demonstrations - and Diem's regime reacted with a brutal crackdown on any and all protest. The trouble began in the city of Hue, where nine unarmed protestors were shot dead or killed with grenades as they complained that they were forbidden to fly a Buddhist flag. Diem accused Buddhists of being secret communists. Soon after, troops poured caustic chemicals over the heads of Buddhists at prayer. On July 7th, American journalists sent to cover the protests were attacked by Diem's secret police. They hadn't counted on David Halberstam of The New York Times, who was much bigger than the Vietnamese policemen and who drove them away in a flurry of well-aimed punches. Now martial law was declared. Buddhist pagodas were assaulted and destroyed, and religious leaders began to disappear. Students who demonstrated in support of the Buddhists were arrested and sent to 'Re-education Camps'.

On June 11th 1963, the first Buddhist monk burned himself to death in Saigon to protest what was happening. His name was Thích Quang Duc. More followed. One member of the ruling South Vietnamese regime said he'd clap the next time he saw a monk immolating himself. Another offered to buy petrol. The Vietnamese First Lady threatened to bring marshmallows. There would be more.

The Kennedy administration started to wake up to reality. They had backed the wrong horse in President Diem. His A.R.V.N. forces were lacklustre in the field at best and Diem had personally told his most senior officers that the real job of the A.R.V.N. was not to attack the Viet Cong but to protect the president and his family at all costs. America was paying $1 million dollars a day to protect a corrupt tyrant from his own people.

In August 1963, Henry Cabot Lodge, the new American ambassador to Vietnam, arrived with a secret agenda. He was to find elements of the South Vietnamese military opposed to Diem and gently, subtly, almost imperceptibly encourage a coup. Diem was officially no longer 'our boy'. There were hopes for a coup against Diem within just weeks of Lodge's arrival but it fell apart due to mutual mistrust. Lodge had to wait until early October for his next chance.

On October 5th 1963, a group of rebel South Vietnamese generals led by Duong Van 'Big' Minh approached Lodge. They wanted assurances that the C.I.A. would not interfere in any coup attempt and that South Vietnam would continue to receive support from America after the coup. The terms were relayed to Kennedy and he agreed them. Kennedy had sanctioned the overthrow of his own man in Vietnam.

As the days to the intended coup started to count down, Kennedy was stricken by a sudden attack of nerves or conscience or both. His brother Robert had been expressing sincere doubts saying, 'We're putting the whole future of the country ... in the hands of someone we don't know very well.' Kennedy's Vice President Lyndon Johnson had always spoken out against the coup. Now Kennedy changed his mind. He ordered Lodge to stop the coup. Lodge in turn said that was impossible – unless Kennedy wanted him to betray the rebel generals to Diem. Like it or not, everything was about to change...

THE COUP

On November 1st 1963, rebel units of the A.V.R.N. surrounded and then assaulted Gia Long Palace in Saigon, home of Diem and his brother Ngo. The fighting was fierce and continued through the night. When the rebels succeeded in breaching the defences of the palace, they discovered that neither the President nor his brother were at home. They had escaped by tunnel during the fighting, dragging several suitcases packed with American

ABOVE LEFT: Lyndon Johnson, President Ngo Dinh Diem and Frederick Nolting, Frederick Nolting. 12th May 1961 | **ABOVE CENTRE:** Hmong ADC company during a mission in Spring 1961 | **ABOVE RIGHT:** Ngo Dinh Diem's body after being shot and killed in the 1963 coup

banknotes. Now, they were actually at a safe house in Cholon.

After fraught negotiations, the brothers agreed to surrender to General Minh on condition of safe passage into exile. They were to be put on a flight out of South Vietnam from Tan Son Nhut Air Base. An armoured car was sent to collect them and they were bundled inside where their arms were tied behind their backs. Nhu complained that he was too important to travel in a mere armoured personnel carrier. On the way to the air base they were both shot dead, most probably by General Minh's personal bodyguard.

Minh didn't try the old 'they were shot trying to escape' gambit. Instead, he suggested that the brothers had killed themselves. Another officer would claim it was all an accident. Forensic evidence and graphic photographs of the body soon dispelled both notions. The brothers had been sprayed with machine gun fire at point blank range and then stabbed numerous times to finish them off. This did not stop South Vietnamese radio from announcing that the brothers had poisoned themselves – which triggered off a wave of celebration amongst the South Vietnamese people. Crowds gathered outside the American Embassy, cheering and gaily waving flags in their spontaneous delight. In South Vietnam, the brothers were buried in secret without ceremony. In Hanoi however, Ho Chi Minh was incredulous when he received the news '*Surely the Americans cannot have been that stupid,*' he said.

THE AMERICAN REACTION

The White House first learned about the deaths of Diem and Nhu on November 3rd, when news filtered through that the brothers had committed suicide. Kennedy was informed at a morning cabinet meeting. He leapt to his feet at the news and those present said he looked utterly shocked and sickened before dashing from the room. He also didn't buy the story that the brothers had committed suicide. Like them, Kennedy was a Catholic and understood that suicide was a mortal sin. Kennedy knew at once that this was an act of cold-blooded murder and – by authorising the coup – he was complicit in it.

Just three weeks later, President John F. Kennedy himself was assassinated in Dallas on November 22nd, 1963.

JOHNSON STEPS UP

Lyndon Baines Johnson was sworn in as the 36th President of the United States on board Air Force One at Dallas Love Airfield on November 22nd 1963 – just two hours after John F. Kennedy had been assassinated. Kennedy's widow Jackie stood beside him. No bible could be found on board the aircraft to be used in the ceremony, so a Catholic pamphlet discovered in Kennedy's desk was pressed into service.

Johnson was a big, rough 6' 4" Texan alpha male. He loved power. He loved control. Politics was a way of getting it. – but somehow he managed to combine ferocious personal ambition with a genuine social conscience . Johnson's aim as president was to bring about what he called 'The Great Society' , a revolution in social justice inside America.

Compared to his social policies, Vietnam was a sideshow – but one he couldn't ignore. Having already had two heart attacks and being in poor health, Johnson was terrified of looking weak both to the American people and the communist bloc. When it came to Vietnam, he would have to look tough.

The Kennedys arrive at Dallas before assasination
INSET: JFK Family leaves after funeral Ceremony

South Vietnam was now in the hands of Big Minh, a general described in one confidential American report as a *'model of lethargy'*. He was overthrown, quite peaceably, on January 30th 1964 and replaced by General Nguyen Khanh. Defence Secretary McNamara flew out to Vietnam to meet the new leader and expressed his support. He returned to recommend that Johnson step up financial and military aid to the new regime. The cost to America now rose to $2 million a day. It's still unknown whether that figure included all the clandestine operations America was running in Vietnam. As McNamara met with the latest regime, C.I.A. backed mercenaries were flying obsolete old American warplanes in strike missions against the Ho Chi Minh Trail. Thousands of new insurgents were pouring south to join the fight now, along with regular N.V.A. troops. Aware of the escalation, the National Security Council suggested to Johnson that bombing North Vietnam might be the only answer. It would certainly be preferable to committing ground troops. He allowed them to make plans but to go no further.

In July 1964, Johnson appointed a new ambassador to South Vietnam - General Maxwell D. Taylor. It was a poisonous job. In his year in Saigon, Taylor would have to deal with no less than five successive Vietnamese regimes as coup followed coup followed coup. That same month, Johnson would also appoint Lt. Gen William C. Westmoreland as U.S. Military Commander in Vietnam.

WESTMORELAND

William Childs Westmoreland was born into a wealthy South Carolina family with a long and proud military tradition on March 26th 1914. He spent his youth proving himself a top Boy Scout.

He attended West Point and left with excellent marks, commanded an artillery unit in North Africa, Sicily, France and Germany during the Second World War and during the Korean War commanded the 187th Airborne Infantry. He took command of the 101st Airborne Division – which would later gain battle honours in Vietnam – in 1956. Those who fought under him generally regarded him as tough but also considerate – a man who valued other men's lives. Enjoying a stellar career, he became the first man ever to reach the rank of major general by the age of 42. He married his wife Kitsy in 1947 and had three children.

In the early 1960s Westmoreland acted as superintendent at West Point before being sent to act as Deputy to the U.S. Military Commander in South Vietnam, General Paul Harkins. He replaced Harkins as commander in the summer of 1964. Before taking up the position, Westmoreland sought the advice of other military men. Legendary General Douglas MacArthur warned him that he might have to use scorched earth tactics and added *'always have plenty of artillery, for the Oriental greatly fears artillery.'* Westmoreland's previous boss, General Harkins, just mumbled a few lines of Kipling about the folly of white men getting involved with the East.

Westmoreland's own assessment of the situation in South Vietnam was grim. He thought that the murder of Diem and the collapse of his regime had *'opened a Pandora's box of political turmoil'*. South Vietnamese forces alone could never hope to win against the united and fanatical communists. American troops would have to do the job.

ABOVE LEFT: General William Westmoreland and President Lyndon B. Johnson at the LBJ Ranch | **ABOVE RIGHT:** U.S. Ambassador to Vietnam Maxwell D. Taylor chats with General William C. Westmoreland, at Tan Son Nhut Airport, Saigon, Vietnam | **OPPOSITE PAGE:** U.S. President Lyndon B. Johnson (r.) meets with the President of France, Charles de Gaulle

THE GULF OF TONKIN

For all I know, our Navy was shooting at whales out there.'

President Johnson, in private conversation, 1965.

During the summer of 1964, President Johnson approved Plan 34A. This allowed C.I.A. operatives to send elite South Vietnamese commandos packed into speedboats to attack sensitive radar sites along the coastline of North Vietnam. An attack on the North itself was obviously very politically sensitive and any American involvement had to be totally denied.

In reality, the U.S. Navy had a number of warships sitting in the Gulf of Tonkin supporting the action under the command of Captain George Stephen Morrison, who happened to be the father of Doors' lead singer Jim Morrison. One of these ships was the destroyer U.S.S. Maddox which used its sophisticated electronic warfare systems to pinpoint the locations of North Vietnamese radar stations. On August 2nd, it was claimed that the Maddox had been attacked by three communist patrol boats while sailing ten miles off the coast of North Vietnam and subjected to both torpedoes and machine gun fire. A single bullet hole was later found and produced as evidence. In response, the nearby U.S. Navy carrier Ticonderoga scrambled four F-8 Crusader jets after the patrol boats, sinking one and damaging the other two (A later enquiry, in 2005, found that the Maddox had initiated hostilities by firing three warning shots at the approaching patrol boats).

President Johnson did not immediately retaliate but instead warned Hanoi of 'grave consequences' if there were to be any further unprovoked attacks.

The next day, the Maddox and another destroyer, the U.S.S. C. Turner Joy, resumed operations even closer in to the North Vietnamese coast. They were acting again in supporting South Vietnamese commandos attacking radar stations. As night fell, a huge thunderstorm rolled across the Gulf of Tonkin, scrambling signals aboard the destroyers. In the confusion, there were reports of numerous North Vietnamese patrol boats closing in on their positions and torpedoes being fired at them. Effectively blind, the two destroyers began blasting away with multiple weapons systems at the perceived threats.

Despite the chaos and confusion – and the lack of any hard evidence of any second attack – the Joint Chiefs of Staff went to Johnson and demanded a retaliatory bombing raid against North Vietnam. Johnson was torn. The last thing he wanted to do was escalate hostilities but with the press having got hold of the story, he could not appear weak either. 1964 was an election year after all. Johnson bit the bullet.

Shortly after, 64 U.S. Navy fighter-bombers - F-8 Crusaders, A-1 Skyraiders, and A-4 Skyhawks - roared off the carriers Ticonderoga and Constellation in Operation Pierce Arrow. F-4B Phantoms flew escort. They attacked an oil storage facility and four North Vietnamese patrol boat bases, sinking or damaging 25 boats. Two jets were shot down and America's first airman captured. He would remain a prisoner until 1973.

Johnson spoke to the public at midnight, an hour after the attacks started. 'Repeated acts of violence against the armed forces of the United States must be met not only with alert defence, but with a positive reply. That reply is being given as I speak tonight...Our response for the present will be limited and fitting...We Americans know, although others appear to forget, the risk of spreading conflict. We still seek no wider war.' Opinion polls the next day showed that he had the approval of 85% of the American public.

The hawks in Johnson's administration seized the moment and started lobbying Congress to give the president far more freedom of action in Vietnam. Their efforts were almost thwarted when one senator got wind of the fact that the Maddox had been part of a clandestine C.I.A. strike mission. Defence

ABOVE LEFT: Admiral George Stephen Morrison, father of Doors lead singer Jim Morrison | **ABOVE CENTRE:** USS Bon Homme Richard (CVA-31) with screen off Vietnam in 1964 | **ABOVE RIGHT:** USS Maddox (DD-731) underway at sea | **RIGHT:** Two Douglas A-4C Skyhawks fly past the anti-submarine carrier USS Kearsarge.

Secretary McNamara had to issue furious assurances that the Navy '...*played absolutely no part in, was not associated with, was not aware of, any South Vietnamese actions, if there were any...*'. In other words, he lied. On August 7th, Congress almost unanimously passed 'The Gulf of Tonkin Resolution'. This gave Johnson the power to take any and all necessary steps to stop further attacks against the U.S. Military without any need to officially declare war.

Those surrounding Johnson who were in favour of escalating involvement in Vietnam had just handed their President a raft of new powers, whether he wanted them or not. Now they began to poke him with a metaphorical stick to use them.

WAITING AND HOPING

Lyndon B. Johnson spent most of the rest of 1964 trying to get himself re-elected as President of the United States and furiously hedging his bets. While trying to appear tough, he was also keen to stress that he was opposed to escalation in Vietnam, promising '*We are not about to send American boys nine or ten thousand miles away from home to do what Asian boys ought to be doing for themselves.*'

On the eve of the vote, Viet Cong guerrillas mortared the air base at Bien Hoa in the early hours of November 1st. Five American servicemen were killed along with two South Vietnamese and five B-57 bombers destroyed. Almost 100 other American and South Vietnamese were wounded. Johnson was pressured to launch an immediate retaliatory air strike against the communist North. He refused. The tactic worked. On November 3rd, he was re-elected President of the United States with a record majority.

In South Vietnam coups and attempted coups seemed to happen all the time. Ambassador Taylor despaired of knowing who was in charge from one month to the next. In December 1964, he finally lost his temper and summoned the latest army officers to seize power - General Khanh and young officers Nguyen Cao Ky and Nguyen Van Thieu – and apparently '*scolded them like naughty schoolboys*'. The new rulers of South Vietnam didn't take too kindly to being addressed like that and complained bitterly to the world's media, accusing America of acting like the Colonialists of old.

On Christmas Eve, Viet Cong guerrillas planted a bomb at the Brinks Hotel in downtown Saigon, which was being used as an officer's residence. It exploded in the bar during 'Happy Hour', killing two Americans and injuring another 58. Voices all around Johnson pressed for a Christmas Day reprisal raid against the North. Again he refused.

And way out in the wilds, in the Central Highlands of Vietnam, 100,000 N.V.A. soldiers had just arrived from an arduous journey down the Ho Chi Minh Trail. As the 23,000 American service personnel now in country celebrated Christmas 1964, they now unknowingly faced a combined force of 170,000 N.V.A. regulars and Viet Cong guerrillas.

1965 would be far from a happy new year.

Charles DeGaulle and Ho Chi Minh are hanged in effigy during the National Shame Day celebration in Saigon, July 1964

Sinh viên
TÂN XÃ
treo cờ
De GAULLE
Hồ chí Minh

Hồ chí Minh

December 24th 1964, Aftermath of the Brinks Hotel Viet Cong bombing in Saigon

1965

ARVN and US Special Forces during operations

CLOSE TO CHAOS

As 1964 turned into 1965, it very soon became increasingly obvious that South Vietnam would collapse within a year if something didn't change.

Over the New Year, almost 200 elite AVRN soldiers lost their lives in a six day battle around the village of Binh Gia. Five American Special Advisors also died in the battle and a further three were reported as M.I.A. A.R.V.N. morale had reached rock bottom. The South Vietnamese government had the power to call up young men for a year's service – but around 30% of all those called up just deserted within six weeks of arriving at barracks. 90,000 A.R.V.N. would desert during 1965.

January 1965 also saw South Vietnam once more shaken by mass demonstrations by Buddhists and students. A young Buddhist girl burned herself to death on the streets of Nha Trang on January 26th. Much of the protests were centred around Tran Van Houng, the puppet civilian President. By the end of the month, he was deposed by General Khanh, the real power in South Vietnam, who promised forthcoming elections to a sceptical nation.

PLEIKU AND FLAMING DART

On February 6th 1965, Viet Cong guerrillas attacked the US air base at Pleiku, in the Central Highlands 250 miles north of Saigon. Nine Americans were killed in the attack and another 76 wounded.

Back in America, Johnson was incandescent. *'I've had enough of this!'* he raged to his security advisors, and retaliated with Operation Flaming Dart, a bombing raid on the N.V.A. camp at Dong Hoi. The attack was carried out by 49 US Navy jets – F-8 Crusaders and A-4 Skyhawks - off the aircraft carriers Coral Sea and Hancock. The

AVRN Soldier

ABOVE LEFT: Twelve year old ARVN Airborne trooper with M-79 grenade launcher | **ABOVE CENTRE:** ARVN Soldier on guard | **ABOVE RIGHT:** Vietnamese army personnel training in the jungle | **BELOW:** Recruitment poster for ARVN Airborne Battalion

Viet Cong retaliated by blowing up the US barracks at Quinhon, killing 23 service personnel. The next day, February 10th, Operation Flaming Dart II saw a combination of land and carrier-based aircraft striking barracks and staging areas in North Vietnam. Three US Navy planes were lost on the mission. From now on, the air war over North Vietnam would be greatly intensified. Johnson's advisors had got their way at last.

In response to the increased American air assault, Soviet leader Kosygin received aggressive requests from the communist North for more military support. Within weeks, sophisticated and deadly SAMs (Surface to Air Missiles) were on their way to the Hanoi regime.

In Saigon, rebel A.R.V.N. officers overthrew General Khanh. Khanh escaped the plotters and threatened to bomb Saigon airport in retaliation unless the rebels conceded. Only the direct influence of General Westmoreland prevented a civil war from breaking out inside South Vietnam. Khanh accepted his time was up and left for a made up government post overseas. Dr. Phan Huy Quat would now lead a government combining both civilian and military men.

General Westmoreland too sensed that his moment had come. On February 22nd, he requested two battalions of U.S. Marines be sent to Vietnam to protect the critical air base at Da Nang. There were, he said, reports of some 6,000 Viet Cong massing in the region ready to assault and overrun the base. Johnson readily agreed, against the direct advice of Ambassador Taylor who warned that the Americans were likely to make the same mistake as the French had done before. In a cruel twist of irony, America had tried to use air power to curb the North Vietnamese and prevent a ground war. Now, they had to send troops in anyway, to protect the very aircraft intended to make ground troops unnecessary.

ROLLING THUNDER GETS ROLLING

The two Flaming Dart air attacks on North Vietnam pointed to a way in which America could bring its superior technology and firepower to bear on the North Vietnamese without getting caught up in a protracted ground war. More air attacks – it was reasoned - would raise both American and South Vietnamese morale, hurt the North Vietnamese war effort, make the war seem unwinnable to the communists and maybe force them to negotiate. It was, on paper, a very attractive looking strategy.

The plans for Operation Rolling Thunder had been drawn up by the American Joint Chiefs of Staff as long ago as August 1964. They had identified a list of 94 targets – mostly parts of the North Vietnamese transport network and which included bridges, rail yards, docks, army barracks and munitions and fuel supply dumps. Now finally, in February 1965, President Johnson gave permission for an eight week limited aerial assault to commence. Much to the dismay of his more aggressive aides and advisors however, Johnson insisted on personally approving each target. There would be no raids on Hanoi itself, and no mining the harbour at strategically vital Haiphong. *'I won't let those air force generals bomb the smallest outhouse...without checking with me,'* he boasted.

On March 2nd, forty F-100 Supersabres roared off the runway at Da Nang airbase. They were joined by twenty B-57s from Tan Son Nhut and forty-four F-105 Thunderchiefs out of Thailand, plus an assortment of support and aerial tankers. Their target - an ammunition dump at Xom Bang, 35 miles into North Vietnam. The Supersabres went in first, tangling with the N.V.A.'s anti-aircraft positions and strafing them with rockets and 20 mike-mike cannon shells. Then in came the first wave of Thunderchiefs on their bombing runs. Unfortunately, scheduling over the target area had become confused, leaving other Thunderchiefs to stack up over the target and get peppered with AA fire as they waited their turn. The B-57s came in last, dropping their entire bomb load in a single pass. A simultaneous mission was flown that night by 19 Vietnamese Air Force (V.N.A.F.) Skyraiders, who dropped 20 tons of bombs on the enemy Quang Khe naval base. Later intelligence evaluations estimated that between 70-80% of the enemy targets had been destroyed. However, five aircraft had been lost in the raid – a much higher figure than anyone had ever expected.

On March 15th, over 100 U.S.A.F. and U.S. Navy jets struck an ammo dump less than 100 miles from Hanoi. The use of napalm was now permitted. Between March 19th and March 25th, solitary U.S.A.F. and V.N.A.F. aircraft were permitted to go hunting – strafing, bombing and rocketing railway locomotives and military trucks along carefully chosen combat routes. Week Three was 'Radar-busting Week' in which US Navy carrier aircraft and U.S.A.F. warplanes out of Thailand went for – and destroyed - nine out of nine Vietnamese radar installations chosen as targets.

The more hawkish members of the US military were singularly unimpressed. One expressed the view that the Hanoi regime had probably no idea that U.S.A.F. and U.S.N. had even been there, while Ambassador Taylor called for a *'mounting crescendo'* of air attacks. Rolling Thunder to date, he sneered, had amounted to little more than *'a few isolated thunderclaps'* as far as the Hanoi regime was concerned.

Johnson compromised – but only a little. Targets could now be chosen more for their military significance. On April 3rd, U.S.N. aircraft attacked and severely damaged the strategic bridge at Dong Thoung, less than 70 miles from Hanoi – and were intercepted by North Vietnamese Mig-15 fighters for the first time. No aircraft were lost on either side. That same day, 46 Thunderchiefs packing bombs and missiles went after the bridge they called Ham Rong – the Dragon's

ABOVE LEFT: Three Republic F-105D Thunderchiefs of the 34th Tactical Fighter Squadron | **ABOVE RIGHT:** Navy Douglas A-4E Skyhawk of Attack Squadron VA-55 Warhorses in flight | **OPPOSITE PAGE:** F-105D Thunderchief fighters refuel from a Boeing KC-135A Stratotanker en route to North Vietnam

Jaw. A vital point on the supply route to the Ho Chi Minh Trail, it was covered with defensive A.A. batteries, which were engaged by F-100 Supersabres as the heavier Thunderchiefs went in. Despite numerous hits, the bridge held. The next day the Thunderchiefs went out again – with bigger bombs. Flying air cover were four F-100 Supersabres. As the Thunderchiefs started their bombing run, a flight of four North Vietnamese MiG-17s bounced them, having successfully evaded the fighter escort. Their cannon fire brought down the first two Thunderchiefs before the MiGs fled for home. Despite this, the surviving Thunderchiefs pressed home their assault. They scored numerous hits but the bridge still held – and would hold for many more years, despite being hit with a total of 12,500 tons of bombs. (It was finally destroyed by new 'Smart Bomb' technology in 1972.)

Despite this notable failure, Operation Rolling Thunder managed to knock out 26 other bridges in just four weeks. What were called 'Armed Reconnaissance' missions were stepped up from three a week to 24 a day, as solitary U.S. aircraft went hunting for trains and lorries to strafe and rocket.

On May 13th, Washington called a temporary halt to Rolling Thunder in the hope that North Vietnam would now negotiate. Instead there was nothing but silence from Hanoi – and the communists used the lull in the bombing to repair the damage done to their infrastructure and to bolster their air defences. Operation Rolling Thunder resumed on May 19th 1964. It would continue rolling, on and off, until November 2nd 1968.

ENTER THE MARINES

To protect its Rolling Thunder air bases in Vietnam from communist attack, America now sent in the Marines. To land Marines on sovereign South Vietnamese soil, America had to gain permission from the South Vietnamese

ABOVE LEFT: Combat operations at Ia Drang Valley, Vietnam, Nov 1965
ABOVE RIGHT: Reconnaissance platoon on Search & Destroy mission
LEFT: A young Marine private waits on the beach during landing

government. Of course, this was a formality, but niceties had to be seen to be done. Permission was asked of the nominal leader Dr. Quat. He agreed – but that was largely irrelevant. The real power in the country - General Nguyen Van Thieu, chief of the Armed Forces Council – was also asked. He too agreed, with one proviso. He asked for the arrival of the Marines to be as quiet, inconspicuous and low key as possible. Westmoreland gave him his word.

On March 8th 1965, the first wave of 3,500 U.S. Marines stormed ashore at China Beach near Da Nang. They were in full combat gear, rifles locked and loaded, leaping into the shallows off landing assault craft and racing up the beach, screaming ferociously. They had been told they might face Viet Cong snipers or even large numbers of guerrillas massing to repel them. There might be mortar fire. There might be V.C. suicide squads with bombs strapped to their chests. As the Marines hit the beach they were ready for anything – except schoolgirls.

Charging up the beach M-14s at the ready, the Marines found themselves confronted by a gaggle of sweet young girls bearing flowers for the soldiers. The Marine commander, Brigadier General Frederick J. Karch, was bedecked in garlands of flowers and mobbed by giggling little girls. A smattering of Vietnamese civilians who just happened to be on the beach looked on bewildered and snapped off shots with their cameras.. General Westmoreland was reported to have buried his head in his hands and described it all as 'appalling'.

It took five days for all 3,500 Marines to make it to shore, accompanied by tons of equipment including a number of tanks, some with flame thrower capabilities. The Viet Cong did eventually materialise and take a few pot-shots at the Marines, but no casualties were reported. Instead, the Marines took up their assigned positions within Da Nang air base and on the surrounding high ground and waited...

Over the next few weeks, the air base saw a flurry of activity. F-4 Phantoms from two Marine Attack Squadrons flew in, along with an aerial reconnaissance detachment and two helicopter squadrons, flying UH-34D Hueys.

Westmoreland re-evaluated the situation. It still wasn't nearly enough.

ESCALATION

'We cannot be defeated by force of arms. We will stand in Vietnam'
President Johnson.

On March 30th, a car bomb in Saigon virtually destroyed the American Embassy. Two Americans were killed, along with nineteen Vietnamese.

On April 1st, Johnson authorised two more battalions of U.S. Marines being despatched to Vietnam, with approximately 20,000 further 'logistics personnel' to provide support. Shortly after, he also agreed to American fighting men being allowed to go out into the countryside and jungles to root out V.C. guerrillas as opposed to playing a purely defensive role or acting only in an advisory capacity. It was a watershed moment.

At the same time, Johnson made what he considered to be generous peace offerings towards Hanoi. At Johns Hopkins University on April 7th, he gave his famous *'Peace Without Conquest'* speech which offered unconditional discussions on peace and massive American economic investment in Vietnam to *'modernize'* the country'. *'Old Ho can't turn that down,'* Johnson said confidently. But Old Ho did. And very quickly.

On April 20th, Johnson's top advisors met in Honolulu. They included McNamara, Westmoreland, General Wheeler, William Bundy, and Ambassador Taylor. The goal was to chart a way forward – and the answer they came up with

ABOVE LEFT: U.S. Marine Corps search and destroy operation south of Chu Lai. Viet Cong casualties stood at 599 killed and six captured | **ABOVE RIGHT:** Officer instructs his men on the best method of destroying enemy bicycles and rice found on a search and destroy mission

was to recommend despatching another 40,000 combat troops to Vietnam. The first elements of U.S. Army combat troops arrived in Vietnam on May 3rd. They comprised some 3500 men of the 173rd Airborne Brigade.

The events of the next two months frankly shook the American administration. On May 11th, South Vietnamese forces were routed by Viet Cong elements in Phuoc Long Province north of Saigon and two days later, the U.S. Special Forces compound there was the scene of savage fighting. Johnson once again tried to get peace talks going, by halting his bombing offensive against the North on May 13th – but the Communists showed no interest. By May 19th, bombing attacks had resumed. On July 1st, the V.C. destroyed three aircraft on the ground at Da Dang air base in a sustained mortar attack, despite the protection of the Marines.

Between July 21st and 28th, Johnson met with his top aides to decide how to respond. At a press conference on July 28th, he told the American people that he would be sending another 44 combat battalions to Vietnam – and that the monthly draft would be doubled to 35,000. He was, he told a shocked nation, responding to Westmoreland's assessment of what was needed in the situation. At the same time he apologised for his actions, saying...

'I do not find it easy to send the flower of our youth, our finest young men, into battle. I have spoken to you today of the divisions and the forces and the battalions and the units, but I know them all – every one. I have seen them in a thousand streets, of a hundred towns, in every state in this union-working and laughing and building - and filled with hope and life. I think I know, too, how their mothers weep and how their families sorrow.'

America had had the Draft in place since 1940. How they used it depended on the world situation. Now Johnson needed more conscripts and the Draft stepped up in pace. Throughout the course of the Vietnam War, around 1/3rd of all American troops would be Draft conscripts. 25% of these would be designated as coming from 'poor' families, 55% from the 'working class' and 20% from the middle class. Those figures meant that the Ghettos would be giving more than their fair share. Richer kids tended to find ways to 'defer' their service, through college or by being needed to support their families. Others used their family influence. The sons of poorer and 'less important' families fled overseas. Future U.S. leaders Bill Clinton and Dick Cheney both managed to dodge the Draft.

On August 4th, Johnson appealed to Congress for an extra $1.7 billion to fund the war effort.

SEARCH AND DESTROY

As soon as he assumed command, General Westmoreland was eager to take the fight to the enemy. He wanted to insert troops into hostile territory by helicopters, hunt down and kill the Viet Cong in the area and then withdraw after achieving a decent body count. He called the tactic 'Search and Destroy'. US troops were to *'find, fix and finish'* the enemy, using a combination of high mobility and superior firepower. Troops in the field – once they had located the

Viet Cong prisoners with their hands tied behind their backs are marched along. Each man is joined by a rope around the neck, as US marines move them along.

enemy – could call on the support of forward artillery fire bases, aircraft or even the big guns of warships patrolling off the coast.

'Search and Destroy' was not a new concept. The French had used it in the last years of the Indochina War. The British had also used it in the early years of the Malayan emergency with varying degrees of success – and criticism. It would never win hearts and minds, but it just might conceivably win wars. There was just one problem. President Johnson didn't want to fight that kind of war – at least until events had escalated so badly that he began to listen more to his military.

On June 26th 1965, Westmoreland finally got permission to assign troops to action in the field. Just two days later, 3,000 men of the 173rd Airborne were dropped into War Zone D, 20 miles north of Saigon, out on the hunt along with 800 Australian troops and a Vietnamese airborne unit. It was a damp squib. The enemy melted away rather than coming out to fight.

Later, it was calculated that less than one per cent of all S&D patrol-level missions conducted during 1967 and 1968 ever resulted in contact with the enemy. When A.R.V.N. troops were involved that figure dropped to less than one tenth of one per cent, leading to American jeers that they were using 'Search and Avoid' tactics. Of the tiny percentage of times when American and communist forces did meet in combat, four out of five times it was the communists who initiated the action. Nevertheless, Westmoreland was not discouraged from his Search and Destroy tactics and continued them in many different ways, from small scale actions to massive air cavalry assaults

From Day One, American troops found their task extremely difficult. The Viet Cong did not wear uniforms and the soldiers had great difficulty telling friend from foe. The language, the customs, even the gestures the Vietnamese people made were incomprehensible. There was frustration at not being able to find the enemy and engage him in a stand up fight. Some soldiers figured they were little more than live bait.

There was a struggle to understand the special needs of jungle warfare – in a country in which 301 out of the 303 native species of snake are venomous – and the frequent use of V.C. booby traps made every moment fraught with tension. The booby traps might range from concealed pits full of snakes or sharpened punji stakes coated in excrement to infect wounds to crude grenades inside tin cans or sophisticated foreign ordnance. Most dreaded of all was the 'Bouncing Betty' mine which, when triggered, would spring up to groin height before spraying out deadly shrapnel that could cripple, disembowel - or emasculate.

Because American troops would very seldom be told to hold an area – they would fly in, search and then be flown out – judging who was winning the war was problematic. Generals and politicians tended to understand victory or defeat in terms of territory gained but that could not be applied to Vietnam. Now Westmoreland adopted the notion of 'Body Count' as the decider. Killing more of them than they kill of you. It was going to be a war of attrition. However, Body Count quickly proved to be a very unreliable system. Troops found out that, if they reported a high body count, they got treats like beer and fresh steaks. So they made it up.

Search and Destroy had another problem. At home in America , S&D missions

Marines roundup Viet Cong suspects in Le My. A South Vietnam Popular Force soldier is in the foreground

A MAG-16 helicopter evacuates Starlight casualties, while a Marine M-48 tank stands guard

became known as 'Zippo Missions' because of graphic TV news reports showing American soldiers torching peasant huts with their Zippo lighters. Burning the meagre shelter and possessions of some of the poorest people on earth while threatening them with machine guns didn't play well on TV. People worked out that 'Search And Destroy' equalled SAD. By 1968, Westmoreland would forbid any further use of the term 'Search and Destroy'.

It was just too provocative.

OPERATION STARLIGHT

They called it Operation Starlight. It was really called Operation Satellite but a U.S. Army clerk mis-typed it and Operation Starlight it became.

On August 18th, the U.S. military launched their first major ground offensive of the war. A force of some 1,500 V.C. had been spotted massing for a surprise attack on the airfield at Chu Lai. The guerrillas were mercilessly pounded by artillery and air strikes before 5,500 U.S. Marines were sent in by helicopter and by sea to finish them off. During the ensuing fight some 45 Marines were killed and a further 120 wounded – but V.C. losses were estimated at over 600. Many more V.C. were rumoured to have died, as the battlefield stank for weeks afterwards, allegedly from all the guerrillas who had died and then rotted in the V.C.'s hidden tunnels - which were never found. The operation was judged a huge success for U.S. forces.

US Marines disembark from an M-113 Armored Personal Carrier and run to the shore

INTO THE LA DRANG VALLEY

On November 14th, U.S. combat troops faced North Vietnamese Army regulars for the first time in the La Drang Valley in the Central Highlands of South Vietnam. The 1st Cavalry Division (airmobile) were choppered into the valley and quickly went on the offensive. During the two day battle, the 1st called upon both intense supporting artillery fire and air support from giant B-52 bombers – the first time these aerial leviathans had ever been deployed in support of ground troops. Under intense pressure, what remained of the N.V.A. units melted away into the jungle, leaving over 2,000 dead. 79 Americans died in the fighting and a further 121 were wounded. La Drang was one of the first battles where the Americans used the concept of 'Body Count' to determine success or failure. They declared victory based on a body count ratio of 10-1.

The taste of victory soon turned to ashes when, on November 17th, 400 men from the 7th Cavalry, sent out on foot to secure a helicopter landing zone, were caught in a deadly N.V.A. ambush. 155 Americans died trying to fight their way out, and a further 124 were wounded.

Whoever had won, the N.V.A. had learned a valuable lesson. America could not use its support artillery and aircraft when the N.V.A. or V.C. closed in on the Americans. The field commander at La Drang, Colonel Nguyen Huu An, advised,

'Move inside the column, grab them by the belt, and thus avoid casualties from the artillery and air.'

CULTURE SHOCK

As more and more American units poured into South Vietnam during 1965, they quickly had a corrosive and corrupting influence on the dirt-poor people of the nation. Americans seemed rich beyond the grasp of the South Vietnamese, and thriving black market shanty

ABOVE: Marines from Battalion Landing Team 3/4, en route to Phu Bai from Da Nang | **LEFT:** Sgt. Dennis Troxel as 'Shotgun Rider' in the door of a Bell UH-1B Huey helicopter

Evacuation of the Vietnamese civilians

towns began to spring up around every American base to part the G.I. from his money. Everything was on sale, from goods stolen from the American PX to drugs, alcohol, tobacco and of course sex.

In Saigon, which was affected perhaps worst of all by the influx, it was said you could even buy a stolen tank or helicopter if you had the cash. By 1966, there were 30,000 prostitutes in the capital alone, many of them forced to provide sex after becoming war refugees. That same year, one in every four G.I.s were discovered to have V.D.

Corruption extended to every level of society, and even once-honest men buckled under the temptation. An A.R.V.N. colonel only earned $70 a month. A mere translator in the field working for the Americans could earn $200. The South Vietnamese military began to pilfer and 'redirect' supplies, to the extent that it compromised them as a fighting force. Officers even 'acquired' part of their soldiers' pay. An average A.R.V.N. soldier earned 1/16th of what an American G.I. did – even if his C.O. didn't take a cut – and the disparity in pay for doing the same dangerous job caused increasing resentment towards the Americans. At senior levels of government, politicians and civil servants connived to get their hands on as much of the $1000 million annual infrastructure budget donated by the U.S. as they could. It was madness.

PROTEST

As the war escalated in Vietnam, so did protests against the war at home.

On August 31st, President Johnson made it a criminal offense to burn a draft card. Anyone doing it could receive a five year jail sentence as well as a $1,000 fine. Despite this, the burning of draft cards in front of news cameras became a very potent symbol of resistance.

October 16th saw co-ordinated mass anti-war rallies in 40 different American cities as well as protests in London, Rome and other world capitals. Just over two weeks later, 25,000 pro-war Americans staged a counter demonstration and marched through Washington D.C., led by decorated veterans of previous American conflicts.

In late November, 35,000 anti-war protesters encircled the White House before marching on to a rally at the Washington Monument. In such a heated atmosphere, it's no wonder the Johnson administration chose to keep secret the latest evaluation of the war from the American people. Defence Secretary McNamara had been on a fact-finding mission to South Vietnam. The American people, he concluded, could expect to see 1,000 American boys return to their hometowns in coffins every single month in 1966. The Johnson administration braced themselves – and General Westmoreland got to be Time Magazine's Man of the Year.

Although meaningless to Buddhists and communists alike, President Johnson declared a second halt to the Rolling Thunder aerial bombardment of North Vietnam for Christmas 1965. In a season of peace and goodwill to all men, the Hanoi regime just strengthened their air defences, rebuilt any damage caused and continued to pump men and munitions down the Ho Chi Minh Trail. They didn't have to worry about courting public opinion. That could be dealt with by fear and firing squad.

By the end of 1965, there were 181,000 U.S. personnel in Vietnam. At the end of 1964 there had been just 23,000.

ABOVE LEFT: Dutch protests at the U.S. consulate against the presence of U.S. troops in Vietnam | **ABOVE CENTRE:** Protesters act out "Saigon Puppet" demonstration in Wichita City | **ABOVE RIGHT:** Protesters around their bonfire after spending the night at the Pentagon's mall entrance | **LEFT:** U.S. Marshals bodily remove one of the protesters during the outbreak of violence at the Pentagon Building

1966

RA-5C Vigilante of Reconnaissance Heavy Attack Squadron RVAH-6 "Fleurs" aboard the aircraft carrier USS Constellation

THE STATE OF THE UNION

By the start of 1966, President Johnson realized that he had let the war in Vietnam slip almost entirely from his grip. He had decided to send in American combat troops. He had let them off the leash and turned them from a defensive force into an offensive force. He had ordered the bombing of the North. He had increased the Draft. He had sent American boys to do the job of Asian boys. This was not the war he had ever envisaged fighting. Now he was splitting America too, trying to keep the patriotic right happy while addressing the concerns of the young and radical left, whom he saw as his more natural constituency.

In his State of the Union address on January 12th 1966, he told the nation, *'Yet, finally, war is always the same. It is young men dying in the fullness of their promise. It is trying to kill a man that you do not even know well enough to hate... therefore, to know war is to know that there is still madness in this world.'* The war was madness – but he was the one ramping it up.

His cessation of the bombing campaign on the North had received nothing but derision from Hanoi. They had no interest in peace. They wanted victory. They did not share Johnson's dilemma in the slightest. In Washington, Johnson was bombarded by dissenting voices. Senator McGovern warned that there was little chance of any peace because America simply didn't understand the complex politics of Vietnam, while the Senate majority leader Mike Mansfield warned that the Vietnam War could inflame and engulf all of the South East Asian peninsula. He went on to point out that a year's fighting in Vietnam had achieved nothing of any significance. And that from a fellow Democrat. The Senate minority leader, Republican Everett Dirksen, attacked Johnson from the opposite direction. He sneered at Johnson's attempts to hold peace talks with the Hanoi regime. What

US President Lyndon B. Johnson

Infantry patrol move towards the last Viet Cong position during Operation Hawthorne

the Republicans wanted, he said, was nothing less than total military victory in Vietnam before any peace talks could even be considered. The Johnson administration was too weak to fight a proper war and should attack the North with more vigour, beginning with a naval blockade of the country. Even Ho Chi Minh himself couldn't resist chipping in, demanding that America recognise his regime as the legitimate government of the South as well as the North.

Meanwhile, Defence Secretary McNamara was strongly recommending an increase in troop strength in Vietnam to over 400,000 by the end of the year – only to have General Westmoreland saying he needed even more men than that to achieve victory by 1967.

By the end of January 1966, Johnson decided to resume Operation Rolling Thunder and unleash U.S. air power against the North once more. Now he was fiercely attacked by his close friend Senator Robert F. Kennedy who said that the bombing put America *'on a road from which there is no turning back, a road that leads to catastrophe for all mankind.'*

OPERATION MASHER

On January 28th 1966, the Americans unleashed Operation Masher, a massive 'Search and Destroy' mission against both V.C. and N.V.A. bases inside South Vietnam, principally around the coastal Bon Son Plain. The operation lasted for 42 days, during which time Johnson delicately changed its name from Masher to White Wing because the former sounded too violent. 228 American soldiers died in the fighting and over 750 were wounded. V.C. and N.V.A. losses were put at 2,389.

Operation Georgia. Marines blow bunkers and tunnels used by the Viet Cong

ABOVE LEFT: South Vietnam Vice President Nguyen Cao Ky and Lyndon B. Johnson | ABOVE CENTRE: B-52F-70-BW Stratofortress from the 320th Bomb Wing dropping Mk 117 750 lb bombs | ABOVE RIGHT: U.S. Air Force Douglas A-1E Skyraider drops a white phosphorus bomb on a Viet Cong postion in South Vietnam

The success of the operation was marred by two atrocities perpetrated by the South Korean ROK Capital Division participating in the assault. In the cluster of villages comprising the Bình An commune, 380 unarmed South Vietnamese civilians were massacred in just one bloody hour of madness on February 26th. Another assault by the same unit on Tây Vinh village saw 67 civilians rounded up and murdered. Just three villagers survived.

A CIVIL WAR WITHIN A CIVIL WAR

South Vietnam was now under the leadership of President Ky, generally considered to be one of the few honest and relatively incorrupt leaders that the country had yet seen.

However, even Ky could not unite South Vietnam. When he dismissed a leading Buddhist general from the A.R.V.N. in March 1966, the country was shaken by a fresh wave of Buddhist riots. Saigon, Da Nang and Hue all saw explosions of public unrest and violence. Ky's grip on power faltered, affecting American military operations. Demands by Vietnamese Catholics that Vietnamese Buddhists needed to be put in their place made tensions worse. By May, A.R.V.N. troops loyal to Ky were attacking rebel A.R.V.N. factions loyal to the Buddhist cause. More Buddhist monks and nuns doused themselves with petrol and burned themselves to death on the streets of the cities. A prominent Buddhist leader, Tri Quang, blamed Johnson for the horrors. All Johnson could do was to call the immolations ' tragic and unnecessary..' Things only quieted down when Ky's regime captured Tri Quang himself.

Viet Cong prisoner captured during Operation Double Eagle

AIR POWER

By the time Johnson had resumed Operation Rolling Thunder, his patience with Hanoi was at an all-time low. In fact, his patience with just about everybody was at an all-time low.

On April 12th 1966, giant B-52 bombers were vectored against North Vietnam for the first time. They struck against power facilities, war support facilities, transportation lines, military complexes, fuel storage, and air defence installations. Each bomber dropped around 100 bombs, from a height of some six miles up. By the end of June, U.S.A.F. and the U.S.N. were striking against oil installations on the very fringes of Hanoi and Haiphong. Despite being egged on by the hawks in his administration, Johnson still refused to bomb Hanoi itself. He knew that such an escalation might bring the North's Soviet and Chinese backers directly into the conflict. Of course they were already there, helping to man anti-aircraft guns and missiles, flying MiG interceptors and training N.V.A. troops – but everyone had to pretend they weren't.

Summer saw U.S. warplanes attacking communist forces in the DMZ – the buffer zone between North and South – for the first time, when an enemy camp and depot suffered six days of intense bombing from B-52s operating out of Guam. It was now estimated that over one half of North Vietnamese oil installations had been attacked and destroyed. On July 15th, U.S. aircraft flew a record total of 121 missions against the North in one day. That record would only last until September 12th, when 500 U.S. warplanes attacked North Vietnamese targets in a single day.

Aside from Rolling Thunder's attacks on the North, the Americans also stepped up strikes against the Ho Chi Minh Trail – but locating enemy forces under the jungle canopy was proving as difficult and frustrating as ever.

OPERATION HASTINGS

In May, intelligence began to reach the Americans that the communists were planning their boldest move of the war to date. They were looking to use a huge force of N.V.A. soldiers – specifically the N.V.A.'s 324-B Division – to seize complete control of Quang Tri Province just south of the DMZ. The N.V.A. were already in place, it was rumoured, and could strike at any time. Westmoreland wanted to go get them, but senior Marine commanders suspected a trap to draw their forces north so that Da Nang would be vulnerable to assault. A reconnaissance team was sent in – and barely escaped with their lives. The area was positively swarming with N.V.A. forces. Two further recon missions confirmed that N.V.A. regulars had crossed the DMZ for the first time and were out for a fight.

On July 15th 1966, a combined force of over 8,500 U.S. Marines supported by 2500 A.R.V.N. moved into to hunt them down. It was the largest combined operation of the war so far. The two sides were locked in ferocious combat until August 3rd. F-4B Phantoms, A-4 Skyhawks, and F-8 Crusaders flew over 100 sorties a day on ground attack missions in support of the Marines, who could also call upon highly accurate and effective artillery support. By the time the N.V.A. had managed to disengage themselves and fled back across the DMZ, 126 Marines had been killed and almost 500 wounded. The A.R.V.N. lost 21 men. N.V.A. losses were estimated to be in the region of 800 dead.

Almost as soon as the Marines had left the area, the N.V.A. returned, building a series of heavily fortified defensive positions while they gathered strength to threaten the coastal areas of Quang Tri. To meet the threat, the Marines quickly launched Operation Prairie. An extra 1500 Marines were shipped in by sea, supported by heavy armour for use in combat outside of jungle areas, and began ruthlessly hunting down N.V.A. positions. The fight waged through August and September comprising mainly of a series of assaults on N.V.A. hillside and hilltop fortifications aided by helicopter gunships and Puff the Magic Dragon- the AC-47 gunship bristling with Gatling Guns. As the monsoons swept in that year, it was clear that the N.V.A. had taken well over a thousand further casualties and were in no position to take over Quang Tri – at least this year.

Later, General Walt described the calibre of the N.V.A. troops his men had encountered. He said, *'We found them well-equipped, well-trained and aggressive to the point of fanaticism. They attacked in massed formations and died by the hundreds'.*

OPERATION ATTLEBORO

As Operation Prairie was raging in Quang Tri, just 60 miles from Saigon, the 9th Viet Cong Division were secretly massing men and supplies for a November offensive. Their hope was to assault the 196th Light Infantry Brigade base at Tay Ninh West, as well as a U.S. Special Forces unit at Suoi Da, northeast of Tay Ninh and catch them completely off guard. The high command in Hanoi, monitoring anti-war protests in America, had decided that killing lots of American soldiers was the key

Operation Hastings. Marines of Company H, 2nd Battalion, 4th Marine Regiment take to the water to join up with their battalion

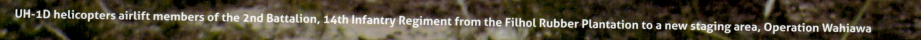
UH-1D helicopters airlift members of the 2nd Battalion, 14th Infantry Regiment from the Filhol Rubber Plantation to a new staging area, Operation Wahiawa

Members of 1st Marine Division carrying their wounded during firefight near southern edge of DMZ

Three young Vietnamese women with rifles on their shoulders

to forcing an American withdrawal.

Their plans were foiled completely by chance. On September 14th, combined U.S. Infantry and South Vietnamese forces numbering some 20,000 men launched Operation Attleboro in Tay Ninh. The area, although heavily forested, was considered to have relatively few enemy guerrillas and the operation was intended to introduce the newly-arrived U.S. Army 196th Light Infantry to Search & Destroy operations with an 'easy' mission.

Initially contact with the enemy was light, but then more and more ammunition dumps and supply caches began to be uncovered. Realising they were about to lose everything, the Viet Cong started to fight back rather than hide. Elements of the 101st N.V.A. Division were rushed in to help them. Over two months of fighting, both the V.C. and N.V.A. forces were dealt a heavy blow. The operation successfully located a huge enemy arms dump hidden in the jungle and this was hailed as a major success. The fighting finally ceased on November 24th by which time 1106 Viet Cong had been been killed and the survivors desperately fled to find refuge in neighbouring Cambodia. American losses were put at 155 dead and 494 wounded.

WAR AND PEACE

Despite the military successes of Attleboro, Prairie and Hastings, President Johnson still searched for a diplomatic solution to the war. In late October 1966, after a meeting with international allies in Manila, he promised to pull all foreign forces out of South Vietnam within six months if the North would withdraw its regular and army forces from the South too. The North showed no interest. Johnson tried another tack, trying to arrange an exchange of POWs and better, more humane treatment

ABOVE: Troops of "A" Company, 1st Air Cavalry Division, checking a villager's home for Viet Cong during patrol | **LEFT:** Girl grieves after 15 were killed when Viet Cong mine exploded on a country road

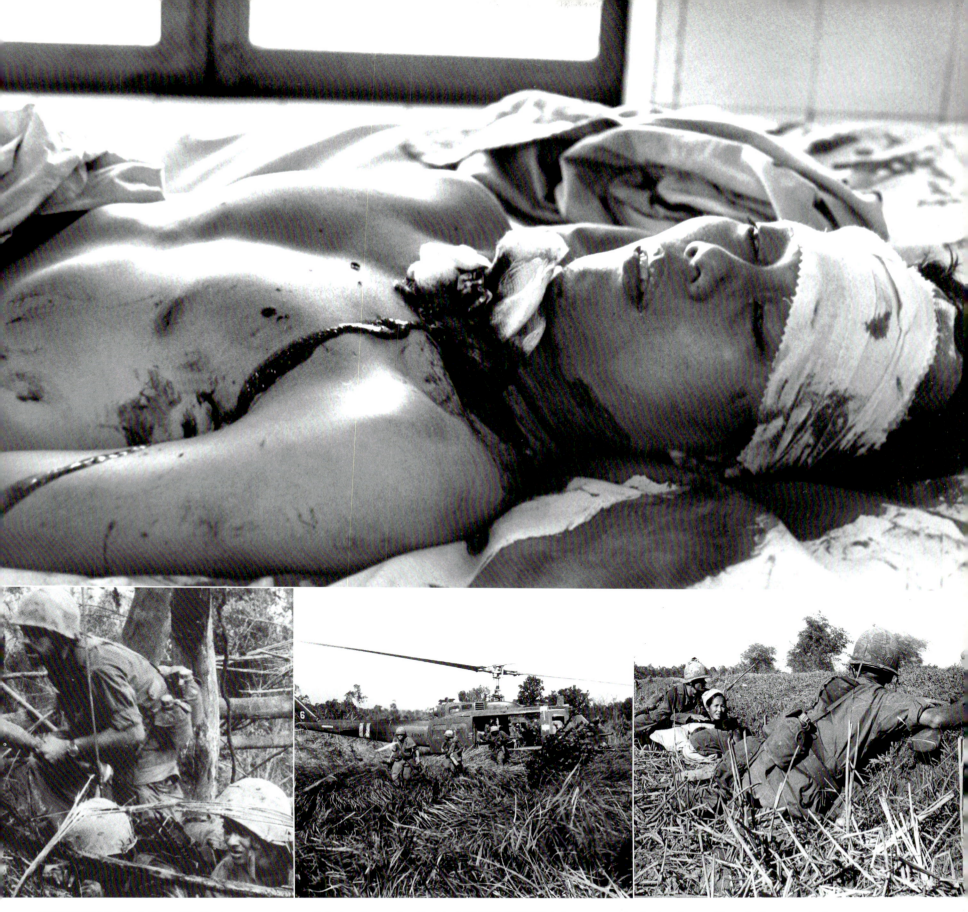

ABOVE LEFT: 3d Battalion, 4th Marines move forward during Operation Prairie | **ABOVE CENTRE:** Infantrymen deploying from a Huey helicopter during Operation Attleboro | **ABOVE RIGHT:** 1st Infantry Division soldier motions to a woman refugee to keep her children's heads down during a fight with Viet Cong | **TOP:** One of 48 wounded by a Viet Cong explosion which killed 14 persons in Saigon

of prisoners on both sides. Again, the communist North showed not the slightest interest. In December 1966, Pope Paul VI tried to get peace talks underway. The Americans listened to his proposals. The North Vietnamese didn't. Meanwhile China got in on the act, denouncing all ideas of peace talks as 'dirty tricks!'

Buoyed up by fresh promises of aid from the Soviet Union, Hanoi was carefully monitoring the anti-war movement in America and calculating that America could never withstand the force of public opinion. On November 7th, Defence Secretary McNamara had been personally confronted by demonstrators when he visited Harvard University. A month later, the American press was full of grudging admissions from U.S., Military commanders that Rolling Thunder strikes may have led to innocent Vietnamese being bombed and killed 'by mistake'. The New York Times was a particularly aggressive critic, accusing U.S.A.F. of *deliberate U.S. attacks on human lives in Nam Dinh City.'* The paper described Nam Dinh as

'a cotton and silk textile town containing nothing of military significance'. This view was countered by a Western diplomat who retorted *'The city in fact contained POL storage, a power plant, and a railroad yard and was surrounded by anti-aircraft guns and missiles;'* No one in the anti-war camp heard a word of the opposing story. Attitudes were hardening and both sides increasingly believed only what they wanted to believe.

As Chairman of the Joint Chiefs of Staff, General Erle G Wheeler would say in March 1967, *'The North Vietnamese don't expect to win a military victory in South Vietnam. They expect to win victory in the war right here in Washington D.C.'*

The war on the ground might be going America's way, but the battle for public opinion was heading in a very different direction. There were now 385,000 U.S. service personnel in Vietnam.

ABOVE: Naval Air station Moffet Field, California. A lone demonstrator protesting the war in Vietnam | OPPOSITE PAGE: Soldiers with dead comrade awaiting the helicopter which will evacuate them from the jungle covered hills in Long Khanh Province

1967

Air Force McDonnell Douglas F-4D-29-MC Phantom of the 435th Tactical Fighter Squadron, 8th Tactical Fighter Wing, armed with two GBU-10s during patrol.

FRUSTRATIONS AND PHANTOMS

On January 2nd 1967, just as another messy New Year ceasefire was ending, 28 U.S.A.F. F-4 Phantom jets finally managed to lure North Vietnamese MiG-21 interceptors into a dogfight over Hanoi. The Phantoms disguised themselves as a flight of slower, weaker, more vulnerable F-105 Thunderchiefs and the MiGs duly came out to play – only to discover themselves facing some of the most formidable fighting aircraft in the world. Seven MiGs were shot down with no losses to the Americans, who utterly dominated the skies during the 15 minute air battle while actual F-105 Thunderchiefs supressed any SAM sites in the area. It was a major blow to the North's air defences as now they were believed to have just nine MiG-21 interceptors left.

Commanders dreamed of going after what remained of the North Vietnamese Air Force and blitzing their five airfields – but they were refused permission. Washington was scared that, if the Vietnamese bases were destroyed, the North might resort to using Chinese military airfields – and Chinese fighter jets might then join Northern interceptors in attacks on American bombers.

Voices started whispering that this was no way to fight a war – and certainly no way to win one...

Back home, speaking at the U.N, Secretary-General U Thant openly questioned whether the eventual fate of South Vietnam really mattered as much as the Americans said it did. In Congress, a growing number of voices – Senator

Wolfpack pilots sweep Colonel Robin Olds away from his F-4 Phantom II

North Vietnamese Air Force MiG-17 pilots walk by their aircraft

Robert Kennedy's amongst them – spoke out in open condemnation of President Johnson's conducting of the war. In turn, he sneered that they were *'Sunshine Patriots'* and *'Nervous Nellies'*. Johnson – not a natural warmonger – was being forced into escalation in defence of his own actions and almost against his will. His ego would not let him bow to his critics or to the regime in Hanoi. Johnson understood that there was little or no chance of the North ever accepting peace. They wanted total victory – and nothing else. They didn't care how many Vietnamese died for them to achieve it – whereas every coffin carried back to America broke more American hearts and weakened its resolve. A long war of attrition suited Hanoi just fine.

OPERATION CEDAR FALLS

Viet Cong guerrillas were now operating quite brazenly almost within the shadow of Saigon. They dominated an area less than 25 miles from the city which became known as the Iron Triangle. The area was, said one commander *'a dagger pointed at the heart of Saigon'*. It was so dangerous that A.R.V.N. forces refused to operate anywhere near it.

On January 8th 1967, in direct response, American forces launched Operation Cedar Falls. This was a massive Search and Destroy mission intended to wipe out V.C. forces operating in the 'Iron Triangle'. The area was rapidly flooded with a force of 16,000 U.S. Troops mixing infantry, armoured cavalry and airborne forces. It was to be the largest American ground operation of the entire conflict, with a further 14,000 A.R.V.N. acting in support.

Unfortunately, due to the usual problem of discerning friend from foe on Search and Destroy missions, the U.S. forces had been given instructions not just to fight any Viet Cong they encountered, but to destroy all the hamlets and villages in the

PFC John Sizemore, C Company, stands guard on Hill 742 as the sun sets in the background

ABOVE LEFT: M113's and M4sa3 tanks deploy between jungle and rubber plantation in Operation Cedar Falls | **ABOVE CENTRE:** Herringbone formation assumed by 3d Squadron, 11th Armored Cavalry, during Operation Cedar Falls | **ABOVE RIGHT:** SGT Ronald A. Payne checks a tunnel for Viet Cong
TOP: UH-1D Huey helicopter prepares for a resupply mission during Operation MacArthur

area and deport the entire Vietnamese population they encountered to 'safer locations' where they could be 'evaluated' as friendly or hostile. They were also to use massive amounts of defoliants in the region to poison the jungle canopy which sheltered and hid V.C. units.

Faced with such overwhelming force, the Viet Cong largely elected to slip away from the area into Cambodia and avoid a fight. What the American ground forces found truly astounded them – a vast network of underground tunnels containing sniper points, command centres, hospitals, ammo dumps, barracks and even cinemas for the screening of propaganda films. Those same tunnels also contained deadly traps – and fanatical Viet Cong fighters who had been 'chosen' to stay behind and prepare deadly underground ambushes.

The American forces gathered on the surface knew that there were V.C. under their feet. They also knew that the tunnels could be full of invaluable V.C. documents and battle plans. They had to get down into the tunnels – but the tunnels were one of the most dangerous fighting environments imaginable. Enter the 'Tunnel Rats'

TUNNEL RATS

Tunnel Rats were an accepted part of American tactics in 1967, and had been since the discovery and infiltration of the Viet Cong Cu Chi tunnel complex in Bin Duoing Province the previous year.

The Tunnel Rats were strictly volunteers. Armed with just a .45 revolver, a knife, a flashlight and (occasionally) a gas mask, they would lower themselves into the tiny, pitch black tunnels – and go hunting. Many were Hispanic Americans, who tended to be smaller than Blacks or Caucasians and could fit better into spaces designed for slight Asian fighters.

Once inside the tunnels, they might encounter an armed V.C. fighter around any bend, or hidden beneath a trapdoor in the tunnel floor or behind a false wall. If they did, whoever got the first shot off – or brought their knife to bear - usually lived. V.C. guerrillas were not the only dangers a Tunnel Rat could expect to encounter as he inched his way forward underground. There were concealed pits containing cobras, boxes of scorpions which would be opened by tripwire, or poisoned punji sticks or nests of stinging ants. Pockets of the tunnels might contain trapped poison gas. The entire complex was one big death trap , to be explored by fingertip or in the narrow beam of a flashlight. Ears were more important than eyes. Instinct more valuable than thought. The secret, revealed one Tunnel Rat, Jack Flowers, was *'Massive fear--that was the key'*. Fear kept you alive.

There were probably no more than 100 'Tunnel Rats' in the American Army during the whole of the war. For most of them, their luck eventually ran out and they died down there. Many of those who survived succumbed to post traumatic stress disorder, reliving the terror and the horror of their experiences in a never-ending loop.

During Cedar Falls, 424 tunnels were found, explored by Tunnel Rats and then destroyed, either by dropping hand grenades into them or by flooding them with acetylene gas and then igniting the gas. Over half a million documents were found in the tunnels or other V.C. structures – some of which revealed the names of V.C. agents operating within Saigon or the local area. Within days, South Vietnamese police and intelligence agents were rounding them up and interrogating them.

Along with the tunnel complexes wiped out, some 1,100 V.C. bunkers were also destroyed and 723 guerrillas killed. The V.C., who privately admitted this had been a major defeat, tried to regain some degree of public face by claiming they had killed over two and a half thousand American servicemen. In reality, actual American and A.R.V.N. losses combined totalled 72. The

ABOVE LEFT: Tunnel Rats, preparing to place charges and make connections for detonation | **ABOVE CENTRE:** U.S. Navy Bell HH-1K Huey helicopter gunner scans the rice paddies below him for signs of enemy movement | **ABOVE RIGHT:** Top of Hill 742, located five miles northeast of Dak To. A purple smoke bomb is ignited to guide in a helicopter

American soldiers use fallen trees for cover during the costly fighting for Hill 875

Americans and A.R.V.N. gathered up their captured booty and moved out of the Iron Triangle in short order.

TWO DAYS LATER...

On the eve of Operation Cedar Falls, Major Allen C. Dixon briefed American news reporters. *'We have two targets, actually,'* he told them. *'There's the Iron Triangle, and then there's the village of Ben Suc. We know there's important V.C. infrastructure there. What we're really after is the infrastructure. We've run several operations in this area before with A.R.V.N. but it's always been hit and run. You go in there, leave the same day and the V.C. are back that night. This time we're really going to do a thorough job of it; we're going to clean out the place completely... The purpose here is to deprive the V.C. of this area for good.'*

Just two days after Operation Cedar Falls ended, the Viet Cong returned to the Iron Triangle. It was as if nothing had changed.

WAR ON THE HOME FRONT

'Hey, Hey LBJ. How many kids did you kill today?'
Anti-war chant.

In Mid-April 1967, America was shaken by some of the largest anti-war demonstrations the country had yet seen. Over 200,000 protestors turned out for mass rallies in San Francisco and New York. Draft cards were publically burned in their hundreds - and the Reverend Martin Luther King grievously wounded President Johnson by pointing out what Johnson knew only too well – that his dreams of progress towards a 'Great Society' were being severely damaged by the Vietnam War.

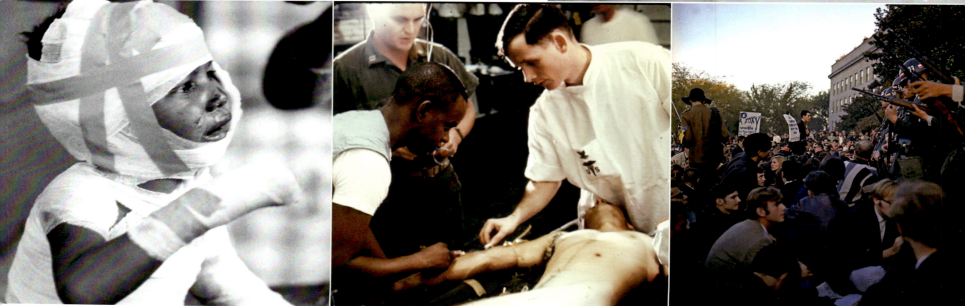

ABOVE LEFT: Infant victim of Dak Son massacre | **ABOVE CENTRE:** Marine Corporal J.A. Holland, who sustained heavy shrapnel wounds in his legs, is given treatment | **ABOVE RIGHT:** More protests at the Pentagon

A Viet Cong prisoner awaits interrogation at the A-109 Special Forces Detachment in Thuong Duc

In Stockholm, Bertrand Russell staged a mock war crimes trial against the American administration for their actions in Vietnam.

On the right, both Nixon and General Westmoreland condemned the anti-war demonstrators. Nixon told them that their actions were only prolonging the war while Westmoreland accused them of giving hope to the enemy - *'hope that he can win politically that which he cannot accomplish militarily.'* On May 13th, a pro-war demonstration some 70,000 strong marched through New York City.

Through the summer and fall of 1967, it seemed to President Johnson that he was hearing nothing but bad news. Westmoreland was saying he needed an extra 200,000 soldiers this year (He would eventually get just 45,000). His peace overtures to North Vietnam were received with absolutely no interest. U.S. troops fighting in the DMZ for the first time suffered heavy losses. A calamitous accident on board the aircraft carrier Forrestal cost the lives of 134 sailors and crew. Two U.S. jets were shot down by the Chinese after straying over their border – and the Rolling Thunder bombing raids on the North were achieving next to nothing. On August 18th, then governor of California Ronald Reagan said that America should get out of Vietnam because there were too many restrictions placed on its bombing missions in the North. Speaking before a senate committee, Defence Secretary McNamara was forced to agree. Despite its cost and despite its intensity, the Rolling Thunder campaign was not significantly damaging the North's ability to wage war on the South. The only way bombing could ever succeed, he commented, was if it was intensified to such an extent that it brought about *'the virtual annihilation of North Vietnam and its people.'*

By October 1967, opinion polls showed that 46% of Americans thought the nation's involvement with Vietnam was a mistake. One of the most common – though least helpful – comments regularly heard from the American public was that the U.S.A. should 'win or get out'. Johnson literally couldn't win.

And then the North attacked.

ABOVE LEFT: Destroying enemy bunkers after assault on Hill 875 | **ABOVE RIGHT:** Infantry descend the side of Hill 742, near Dak To | **LEFT:** American soldiers looking tired and exhausted during the costly fighting for Hill 875.

BORDER WARS

When the North Vietnamese Army came out to fight in mid-September 1967, it came in force. Regiment-sized units began to strike south in sustained assaults rather than in hit-and-run raids.

At Con Thien, just two miles south of the DMZ in Quang Tri Province, a U.S. Marine hilltop base found itself under siege and under ferocious bombardment from artillery and mortars. In the resulting artillery duel, the base received 42,000 rounds of incoming fire. American units fired back some 281,000 rounds in response. Pressure on the base became so intense that General Westmoreland had to launch Operation Neutralize to end it. Giant B-52 bombers and other U.S. warplanes flew almost 4,000 attack sorties against the N.V.A.'s artillery positions. After seven weeks, the N.V.A. disengaged with an estimate of some 2.000 losses.

Even as the high altitude B-52s were trying to relieve the base at Con Thien, a regiment of N.V.A. struck at Song Be, the capital of Phuoc Long Province. The assault lasted for several days but the attackers eventually fell back.

At the end of October, another N.V.A. regiment attempted to overrun a U.S. Special Forces base at Loc Ninh, in Binh Long Province. Elements of the American 1st Infantry Division were called in to provide assistance to the Special Forces personnel and, after a battle lasting some ten days, the surviving N.V.A. were forced to flee into Cambodia, leaving 850 dead behind. American casualties amounted to just 50 men.

The most intense fighting of the entire 'Border War' of 1967, however, was around Dak To, in Kon Tum Province, in the Central Highlands area. The area around Dak To had been volatile all year. The 4th Infantry Division had reported a number of heavy contacts with enemy forces and there had even been fears expressed that the base could be overrun. In response, two battalions of the 173rd Airborne were brought in on June 10th to conduct Operation Greeley, a Search and Destroy mission in deeply hostile mountain and jungle terrain. The operation was a disaster. A company of American Airborne troops were ambushed by a battalion of N.V.A. regulars and pinned down. Other American units battling to reach them were defeated by the terrain. The N.V.A. came in close, which meant the besieged company couldn't call on air or artillery support for fear of hitting their own position. After a day and night spent fighting to stay alive, the soldiers suddenly found that the N.V.A. had disengaged. Out of the original company strength of 137 men, 76 were now dead and a further 23 wounded. Only 15 N.V.A. bodies were found at the site of the ambush. In response, the 173rd were reinforced in the area with elements of the 1st Air Cav and an elite A.R.V.N. force. There were more ambushes, more heavy losses but – by August 1967 – it appeared that the N.V.A. had withdrawn.

At the start of November 1967, a defector from the N.V.A. told the Americans the North Vietnamese were back in Dak To and were planning a major attack from the jungle. They had managed to infiltrate some 6,000 men into the area with ammunition and supplies while constructing an elaborate fortified bunker and trench system under the American's noses. To face them, the Americans hastily assembled a fighting force comprising elements of the 4th Infantry Division and the 173rd, two 1st Air Cav battalions, four battalions of the A.R.V.N. 42nd Regiment and the A.R.V.N. 2nd and 3rd Airborne Battalions.

Operation MacArthur was launched. It mainly consisted of American and A.R.V.N.

Marines of Company E, 2nd Battalion, 9th Marines, Evacuate while under heavy fire with NVAs within the DMZ

units heading out into the jungle and mountainous terrain until they were stopped by an N.V.A. bunker complex. Then they would call in artillery or close air support to take it out. If the support failed to do the job, the troops would have to storm the fortifications and do the job the hard way, with grenades, bayonets and some of the most intense hand-to-hand fighting seen during the entire war.

Elements of the N.V.A. would also launch their own attacks on areas where they saw the Americans had let their guard down. By November 12th, the N.V.A. were in a position to launch almost nightly rocket attacks against the Dak To base. On November 15th, a combined rocket and mortar attack almost devastated the base. Two C-130 transports were caught on the ground and destroyed. Ammunition caches and fuel dumps were hit with unerring accuracy but it was the round that slammed into a store full of C-4 plastic explosives that set off the largest explosion ever recorded during the war. It's claimed that camp personnel a full mile away were hurled off their feet by the force of the blast. It was a rare moment of triumph for the N.V.A.. For the most part, Operation MacArthur proved very successful in driving them out and by the end of November most had slipped away over the border to Laos or Cambodia where the Americans couldn't follow. The Americans had lost some 376 men and 40 helicopters in the fighting around Dak To and the A.R.V.N. 73. No one really knows how many the N.V.A. lost. They did not issue figures and the American body count of 1,644 is regarded as highly suspicious.

At the end of 1967's 'Border War' the Americans, had they wanted to, could have claimed a major victory. The N.V.A. had lost every battle. Even allowing for the corruption in body count figures, N.V.A. losses had to have hurt the enemy. In the end, the enemy had fled the field. There was, however, no crowing from the U.S. Military. They were more baffled than elated. Why had the North launched the offensive along the border? What was so important about this particular part of the countryside?

The N.V.A. knew exactly why they had launched the attacks and – early in 1968 – the Americans would discover the reasons too.

JUST ANOTHER WINTER

The events of the winter of 1967 were – in the main – depressingly predictable. President Johnson made yet more peace overtures to the North Vietnamese who rebuffed them. 55,000 protestors marched on the Pentagon and radicals in London tried to storm the U.S. Embassy there. The celebrity doctor Benjamin Spock got himself arrested during four days of continuous anti-war protests in New York. Film of the protests were shown on giant screens in Hanoi. Johnson told the American people that they were winning the war and making progress. General Westmoreland flexed his muscles in the pages of Time magazine and talked tough. *'I hope they try something,'* he said, *'because we are looking for a fight.'* General Wheeler expressed his concern that the North Vietnamese were banking on a new American administration to pull out of Vietnam rather than a military victory. No one remembered that General Westmoreland had promised victory by 1967. Yet another Christmas truce brought a temporary halt to bombs raining down on North Vietnam.

And somewhere in amongst it all Defence Secretary Robert McNamara resigned. He had lost his faith – and thought that the war effort had lost its way. In private, Johnson described McNamara as *'cracking up'*.

There were now 486,000 U.S. personnel in Vietnam.

1st Battalion, 16th Infantry Medic, looks out for Medevac helicopter to evacuate wounded

1968

Soldiers of the 1. Cavalry Division moving towards Khe Sanh Combat Base during Operation Pegasus

KHE SANH

Khe Sanh was a large combat base and airfield in Quang Tri Province just seven miles from the border with Laos and 14 miles from the DMZ, permanently manned by U.S. Marines. It was ¼ mile wide and ½ mile long. Westmoreland had recognised its strategic significance in the mid-1960s and had hoped to use it as a staging post to raid Laos and severely disrupt the Ho Chi Minh supply trail in the area. Political expediency had never allowed him to do so.

There had been fighting around Khe Sanh since late April 1967, when Marine patrols stumbled across elements of the N.V.A. trying to secretly take up positions in the hills around the base. It was, the Marines suspected, a prelude to an attack in some force. The Marines succeeded in driving the N.V.A. off three strategically important hills close to the base, but only at the cost of some 155 killed and another 425 wounded. N.V.A. losses were estimated at just below one thousand dead. Having won the hills, the Marines then decided to set up permanent bases on them to prevent the enemy returning.

At the very start of January 1968, aerial patrols reported nothing unusual in the vicinity of Khe Sanh – but new acoustic sensors planted in outlying areas started picking up movement – and lots of it. Sensors were going off like crazy all around the perimeter. Khe Sanh was being surrounded. Now snipers began to pick off Marines as they went out on patrol and rumours started to circulated that there were up to 80,000 N.V.A. regulars out there just waiting for their moment. No one said anything to the men, but they knew something big was up when reinforcements started to arrive and orders were given to dig in and hold. There was to be no retreat. There was nowhere to retreat to. More clued up Marines started to think of the French at Dien Bien Phu. Others thought of Custer's Last Stand.

3,500 US Marines and 2,100 A.R.V.N. rangers sat and waited, dug in deep. The

General William C. Westmoreland

U.S. Marines head into combat after being airlifted to Ca Lu Combat Base on Highway 9 east of Khe Sanh

bombardment started on January 21st at dawn, 300 rounds of mortar shells and rockets that killed 18 Marines and wounded forty. Over 1500 tons of high explosives detonated when the N.V.A. artillery targeted Khe Sanh's main ammunition dump. An outlying post on Hill 861 was hit by a human wave of 300 N.V.A. troops. They were repulsed only by heavy hand to hand fighting. Another 300 N.V.A. hit the village of Khe Sanh. They met heavy resistance but succeeded in taking the village, while survivors raced for safety to Khe Sanh base.

On January 24th 100mm and 152mm artillery – the N.V.A.'s so-called 'Steel Elephants' - began a simultaneous softening up process on both the outlying hill forts and the main base itself. They had every target meticulously mapped out – whereas the Americans had huge difficulty in finding the enemy gun positions when they returned fire. Despite being able to fire back 20 shells for every incoming round, the American defences were largely ineffective. Many N.V.A. guns were hidden in cave formations in the hills.

Now US aircraft dropped enhanced acoustic sensors and directed massive aerial firepower against the encircling N.V.A. forces. Opertion Niagra II blitzed suspected N.V.A. positions, turning jungle and thickly forested hillsides into little more than heavily cratered fields of stubble. On any typical day, some 350 fighter-bombers would be flying strike sorties against the N.V.A., together with as many as 60 B-52 heavy bombers flying high altitude bombing runs. The Americans at Khe Sanh were particularly nervous of the B-52s strikes, fearing a friendly fire incident and any such drops were forbidden within 2 miles of friendly forces. This was changed to just ¾ mile from friendlies after some convincing demonstrations. The B-52s were pulverising the enemy – one dazed and wounded N.V.A. captive at the time claimed that ¾ of his entire regiment had been blown to hell in a single B-52 strike – but it was still not enough.

Two soldiers emerge from the rear of a helicopter that's just landed at the Khe Sanh base

The N.V.A. just kept coming.

The encirclement of Khe Sanh rapidly reduced the White House to a state of panic. They saw the comparison to Dien Bien Phu all too clearly – and heard rumours that the victor of Dien Bien Phu – General Giap – had taken personal charge of operations around the base. Only Westmoreland couldn't see any close comparison. He'd chosen Khe Sanh for a reason. Unlike Dien Bien Phu, there were no significant pockets of Vietnamese civilians around for many miles. Khe Sanh was the perfect place to drop a few low yield thermonuclear weapons...

The eyes of the world were on Khe Sanh. Every day it seemed, cargo planes and choppers were bringing fresh loads of supplies, ammo – and journalists to cover the story. Everyone was looking north up to the DMZ -

which was just what the Hanoi regime wanted them to do.

TET

'Crack the Sky, Shake the Earth'

Instructions given to Viet Cong guerrillas on the eve of Tet 1968.

Tet is the Vietnamese New Year. The nation shares it with the Chinese. It's the most important holiday in Vietnam, a time for visiting family. Special meals are cooked, money given to children and the elderly and visits paid to shrines or the graves of ancestors. It's a time of peace.

On the eve of Tet 1968, the Viet Cong in South Vietnam launched the largest offensive of the entire war, coming out of hiding and attacking seemingly everywhere. This is what it had all being leading to. All the actions in the north

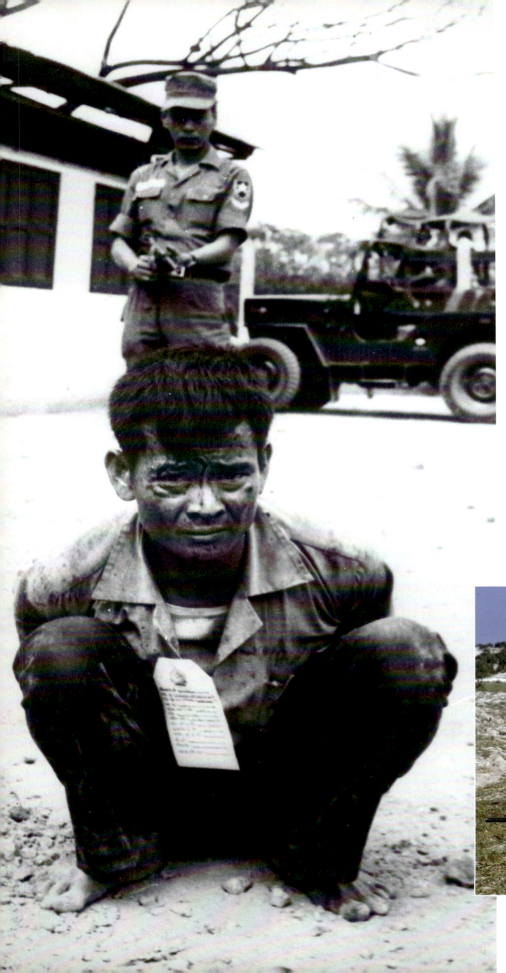

ABOVE: Battle of Hamo Village During the Tet Offensive | **LEFT:** Young Viet cong, awaits interrogation during the festive Tet holiday period

– the border wars, Khe Sanh – they had all been a distraction. As the Americans looked North, the Viet Cong were preparing in the heart of the South, including the capital Saigon.

80,000 Viet Cong guerrillas and N.V.A. infiltrators struck when the South Vietnamese authorities were least prepared. Almost half of the A.R.V.N. were on leave, spending time with their families. Americans were anticipating a few days of comparative peace. After all, the Hanoi Regime had officially announced a Tet truce. They had, of course, lied. The Viet Cong hit over 100 different towns and cities throughout South Vietnam almost simultaneously. Suddenly, the enemy was everywhere.

The first attacks came just after midnight on January 30th. Some ten target towns were hit, first by mortars and rockets and then groups of V.C. fighters looking to take out strategic local targets. Despite being caught by surprise, local A.R.V.N. and police units acquitted themselves well and almost every single V.C. attack failed. Throughout the night word started to spread up the U.S. Chain of Command. Westmoreland was told to brace for many, many more attacks in the next twenty four hours. As American troops were put on alert, the U.S. desperately prepared to steel itself for whatever was to come.

The first reports of V.C. attacks on Saigon started to come in just after 3am and grew in the hours to dawn. The 4,000 V.C. in Saigon had six major targets, including the national radio station and the U.S. Embassy. They also launched battalion strength attacks on the central police station and armoured and artillery headquarters. Small groups were given the addresses of senior civil servants and military officers and sent to kill them in their beds

Guerrillas managed to seize the radio station but could not play their taped speech from Ho Chi Minh because the authorities cut off their ability to broadcast. At the U.S. Embassy, an extraordinary sight played out right in front of the TV news crews. A team of sappers some 19 strong managed to blow a hole in the wall of the embassy grounds, but their attack fell to pieces when their commanding officer was killed early in the engagement and they found their way into the embassy blocked by Marines, CIA operatives, diplomats and ordinary American civil servants grabbing whatever firearms they could reach and blasting back at the V.C.. The surviving guerillas just roamed portions of the grounds until they were hunted down and killed one by one by American reinforcements. Five embassy personnel died in the fighting. Westmoreland, who had turned up towards the end of events, got on the phone to Washington and told them that this was a *'relatively small incident'* and not to panic.

In just a few short hours that morning, most of the V.C. attacks around Saigon City Centre had been crushed. The heaviest fighting remained in Cholon, Saigon's Chinatown, where the V.C. could count on support from the Chinese residents. The civilians were forced to flee as fierce house to house fighting erupted between the A.R.V.N. and V.C. guerrillas. Large areas caught fire. By the end of the first day, five U.S. Battalions were street fighting in Saigon, attacking pockets of pinned down guerrillas. The most stubborn pockets of resistance would be blown to pieces by U.S. ground attack jets.

To prevent the besieged V.C. in Saigon from being reinforced or rescued, local outlying towns known to be sympathetic to the communists were ruthlessly attacked from the air, causing a stream of refugees and well as countless casualties. It was during these operations against one such town, Ben Tre that an American officer coined the immortal phrase, *'we had to destroy it to save it'*.

Tet was very largely over within just ten days. It was nothing less than a stunning victory for U.S. forces, the Vietnamese police and A.R.V.N. units. Westmoreland claimed they had killed over 37,000 enemy combatants and – while any U.S. body count needs to be treated with suspicion – it is certain that Tet was devastating to the Viet Cong. More enemy combatants had been killed in a week than America had lost combat troops in the entire conflict. It was a

ABOVE LEFT: ARVN Rangers defend Saigon during the Tet Offensive **ABOVE RIGHT:** SFC Howard C. Breedlove receives medical attention from 2Lt. Richard M. Griffith on Plantation Rd. in Gia Dinh, a suburb of Saigon.

defeat they never recovered from. General Giap – the architect of Tet – had hoped the Southern masses would rise up to support the guerrillas. They most certainly hadn't. But Tet was also, in the eyes of many, the moment the North won the Vietnam War and demonstrated that the war could not be waged – or judged – in any conventional sense.

American TV viewers could not believe that the enemy had been capable of launching such a huge scale attack with such force. They had been told by their leaders that America was winning the war in Vietnam – but it seemed the North could conjure vast new peasant armies and resources out of nowhere. In his news room, America's most revered news reporter Walter Cronkite was overheard saying, 'What the hell is going on? I thought we were winning this war'.

Tet may have been won, but the war obviously was far from won. And America was rapidly growing tired of the fight. On February 2nd, President Johnson publically pronounced the Tet Offensive, 'a complete failure' but in private he was beginning to have extreme doubts about the viability of winning the war. Westmoreland's response was to call for a further 200,000 American troops. In return, he would shortly get his own marching orders.

And it wasn't as if the fighting had stopped. Americans were still fearful of the fate of the Marines trapped at Khe Sanh – and apprehensive of the conflagration just about to flare up in Hue...

HUE

Hue was South Vietnam's second city, a rich and refined treasure of lush history and exotic beauty sitting astride the Perfumed River. This was the Imperial City, a centre of culture and learning. It was also the target of a mixed communist force of 12,000 V.C. and N.V.A. as the Tet Offensive erupted. The city was only lightly defended – despite being just 30 miles south of the DMZ - and captured with very little effort. Recapturing the city would see some of the bloodiest street fighting of the entire war.

As Hue fell to the communists, guerrilla units scoured the city for civil servants, teachers and religious leaders. They were then executed en masse, by pistol, machine gun, bayonet and being buried alive. Later, American units would discover almost 3,000 bodies in pits. Another 3,000 civilians were reported as missing. Years later, mass graves were still being unearthed in the city. When not hunting down and murdering civilians, the communists took the opportunity to destroy many of the city's beautiful temples, palaces and monuments for being bourgeois . They then dug in and waited for the Americans and A.R.V.N. to arrive.

The V.C. and N.V.A. had not succeeded in driving all of their enemies completely from the city and the counter-attacks began almost immediately, with elements of the U.S. Army, Marine Corps and A.R.V.N. working together to dislodge the communists. There were immediate problems. The strength of the communists was underestimated, and Westmoreland was unwilling initially to pull resources away from the siege still going on at Khe Sanh. There was also reluctance to use armour, artillery and aircraft, due to the priceless treasures and architecture that made the city world famous. All these considerations would eventually have to be discarded to achieve victory; Most of the fighting

A fearless youngster oblivious to danger stands alongside a crouching South Vietnamese soldier in a village street

was over by 10th February, leaving a hard-core of communist troops in the heart of the city around a historic fortress called the Citadel. It took almost two weeks of bitter house to house, street to street fighting to dislodge them and required amphibious assaults, tank support and numerous airstrikes on well dug-in enemy strongpoints in the heart of the city. Progress might be measured in as little as 200 yards of ground a day, as thousands of years of history dissolved under high explosives. It was a particularly difficult fight for the Marines, who were not trained for close-in urban fighting and who had to make up their battle tactics largely as they went, with a good degree of trial and error.

It was another assured win for America and its allies. Over 5,000 V.C. and N.V.A. were said to lie dead in the dusty ruins – and a further 3,000 were thought to have been killed by the 1st Cav and 101st Airborne in support operations nearby. For their part, America had lost 147 Marines, 74 regular army and the A.R.V.N. units suffered 384 killed and 1,800 wounded. To save Hue, the Americans and South Vietnamese had practically had to destroy it. 40% of the entire city had been reduced to rubble and 116,000 out of 140,000 residents made homeless. As the Americans withdrew, elements of A.R.V.N. went on an orgy of looting or started rounding up known communist sympathisers and murdering them.

Graphic images of the close quarter fighting in the streets of Hue had made it onto the nightly news broadcasts and were met with incredulity and horror in millions of American homes. If this was what war looked like, a lot of Americans didn't want it.

MY LAI

**'Everyone in my family was killed in the My Lai massacre —
my mother, my father, my brother and three sisters. They threw me
into a ditch full of dead bodies. I was covered with blood and brains'**
Testimony of an 8-year-old Vietnamese girl.

Throughout February and March of 1968, Charlie Company, 1st Battalion, 20th Infantry had been operating deep in Indian Country on a Search and Destroy mission against the Viet Cong. The area was lethal, riddled with booby traps and anti-personnel mines. The Viet Cong seemed to be everywhere, ambushing, killing and then slipping away again. Word was, the local villagers were hiding them in their hamlets. Charlie Company had suffered numerous losses – and by the time one of its platoons, led by Lieutenant William Calley, sighted two small quiet hamlets collectively called My Lai-4, the men were more than ready for some serious payback.

Calley had received orders from his CO to *'go in there aggressively, close with the enemy and wipe them out for good'*. On March 15th, Charlie Company's Captain Ernest Medina told the men that civilians would not be present at My Lai. They would be at market. Anyone they found there was to be considered V.C. . He concluded his pep talk saying:

'They're all V.C., now go and get them' .

Dr. Howe treats the wounds of Private First Class D. A. Crum, "H" Company, 2nd Battalion, Fifth Marine Regiment, during Operation Hue City.

On March 16th, 1st Platoon entered the village. It was 7.30 am and the people had not yet got ready for market. As they came in, the soldiers fired on villagers working out in the paddy fields and began rounding others up. No one knows how or why the killing started. One witness said he saw a soldier stab a villager with a bayonet, before pushing another into the village well and throwing in a live grenade after him. Twenty women and children discovered praying beside their humble temple were all summarily executed with shots to the head as they begged for their lives.

Another 80 villagers were forced into an irrigation ditch. As they begged for mercy, they were machine gunned. Lieutenant Calley was reported to have joined in the firing himself. Witnesses said that particular attention was paid to machine gunning women with babies in their arms *because they might be concealing grenades'*. When the firing died down, toddlers who had survived under their mothers' bodies began to crawl free. They were singled out and shot one by one. One soldier fired his M-79 grenade launcher directly into a pile of bodies where some were still alive. Elsewhere in the village, huts were set on fire and the occupants mown down as they fled the flames. Women and children were singled out to be gang-raped and then executed. Not one shot was fired at the Americans.

Flying Close Air Support in his Huey over the scene, Warrant Officer Hugh Thompson Junior landed his helicopter to help evacuate any wounded – and found himself caught up in what increasingly seemed to be utter madness. Wounded civilians were he was told *'being put out of their misery'*. When he confronted Calley, the Lieutenant said that he was *'just following orders'*. As Thompson took off again, he saw a soldier shooting a wounded civilian, a woman being kicked to the ground and executed and a group of soldiers threatening civilians huddled in a bunker. Thompson set his Huey down again and went to

ABOVE : Aftermath of the My Lai massacre | **LEFT:** The old and the young flee Tet offensive fighting in Hue

intervene. He told his own crew to fire on Calley's men if they tried to stop him. Thompson prevented the soldiers from lobbing grenades into the bunker and led the civilians – comprised entirely of women, children and elderly people to his helicopter. He and his crew then evacuated them to safety in two groups. On his final flight over the area, Thompson rescued a four year old girl from a ditch full of bodies.

As soon as he got back to base, Thompson reported the massacre. His claims reached the ears of the CO of Charlie Company and there was a call to 'knock off the killings'. Other operations were soon suspended, and possibly hundreds of other lives were saved. For his actions, Thompson was awarded the Distinguished Flying Cross. He threw it away in disgust. When he and his crew tried to bring the massacre to light, they were denounced by some U.S. politicians as 'traitors'.

In the immediate aftermath, there were vague references to civilians accidentally having been killed but also elation at killing 128 Viet Cong. General Westmoreland personally sent his congratulations to the unit on 'an outstanding job'. Stories of the massacre though refused to go away. Within 18 months what had happened at My Lai was common knowledge. In 1970, the trials began. All senior officers were absolved of any responsibility. Twenty six soldiers were charged with criminal offenses. None were convicted. Lieutenant William Calley however was found guilty of murdering 22 civilians and sentenced to life imprisonment. In the event, he served just three and a half years under house arrest until personal intervention by President Nixon. Calley expressed regret in 2009.

In May 1970, an anonymous sergeant wrote a personal letter to General Westmoreland. In it, he claimed that during 1968-9, there had been 'a My Lai each month for over a year'. We may never know about them.

RETURN TO KHE SANH

'For those who fight for it, life has a flavour the sheltered never know'
found written on a Marines noticeboard at Khe Sanh, 1968.

As Hue was finally relieved in the first days of March 1968, President Johnson's old friend and new U.S. Secretary of Defence, Clark Clifford, had a quiet word in his ear. Very gently he said, *'The time has come to decide where we go from here'.* There could be no mistaking what he meant.

Clifford had just completed a study on the situation in Vietnam and had just discovered – to his utter shock and bewilderment – that there was no plan for victory. He, like Johnson, had just lived through the traumatic weeks of the events of Tet and the relief of Hue and the President had a hundred and one other things to deal with. Graphic pictures of a Viet Cong guerrilla being executed with a pistol to his head by South Vietnam's police chief General Nguyen Ngoc had made the front pages of newspapers around the world. (No one cared that the general had just witnessed one of his closest friends being murdered by the same V.C. just minutes before). General Westmoreland was pressing hard for his extra 200,000 troops and – when he didn't get his way immediately – had started leaking his dissatisfaction to the New York Times. World leaders, including Harold Wilson and Charles de Gaulle, had ganged up with U.N. General Secretary U-Thant to call for an end to the bombing of the North in the frankly naive hope that the Hanoi regime might soften. Intelligence sources from Vietnam claimed that all the refugees caused by the Tet fighting had shifted hearts and minds away from America. The Senate Foreign Relations Committee was sniffing around the truth behind the Gulf of Tonkin incident. The military were looking to expand the war into Laos and Cambodia and 48 U.S. soldiers had been killed in a single ambush just a few miles from Tansonnhut air base.

ABOVE LEFT: Casualty during the My Lai massacre | **ABOVE RIGHT:** Unidentified body in well. My Lai, March 16th 1968

A Viet Cong base camp being burned down.

Private First Class David Sletten, medic, Company B, !st Battalion, 27th Infantry, 25th Infantry Division, in a three-man assault boat Operation Tong Thang

In all the whirling chaos, all the voices with different competing agendas, all the bad news and good boys in body bags, it was perhaps the potential fate of Khe Sanh that scared Johnson the most. Johnson had had three giant TV sets installed in the oval office so that he didn't miss a minute of the news, and there was a detailed diorama of the setup at Khe Sanh in the White House basement on which he could follow the progress of events. Johnson was like a man possessed, demanding papers signed in blood from his generals that Khe Sanh would not fall under any circumstance. Westmoreland told him he had nothing to worry about.

The battle at Khe Sanh had been waging all through the events of Tet and the battle for Hue. The N.V.A. had actually used Soviet-built light tanks to overrun the special forces camp at Lang Vei close to Khe Sanh on February 9th. The main base was clinging on tenaciously as were the outlying hill posts but the N.V.A. was keeping up the pressure with frequent mortar barrages and guerrilla-style raids rather than mass assaults. Marine patrols were frequently ambushed and large artillery pieces situated over the border in neutral Laos could land as many as 100 shells a day on the beleaguered Marines. During March the main base's ammo dump was hit and detonated for a second time.

The U.S. forces struck back with 300-400 airstrikes against the N.V.A. every day, homing in on them with their acoustic sensors. By night the N.V.A. would dig new trench lines closer to the base. By day, fighter-bombers would sweep in and burn them out with napalm.

During the fighting, the isolated outlying hill forts were kept supplied by a technique known as the 'Super Gaggle'. A-4-Skyhawks would launch ferocious ground attacks on nearby N.V.A. positions, supressing their fire as a dozen or more helicopters came in to briefly touch down and dump fresh supplies. The main base was supplied by fast in-and-out runs by larger transport aircraft and paradrops.

In April 1968, a relief force combining units of Marines, Army and A.R.V.N. finally succeeded in reopening Route 9 and sending in ground convoys as part of Operation Pegasus. They were dangerous supply runs, but meant that the base at Khe Sanh could now be sent heavier equipment than could be air dropped. The whole idea of having been 'relieved' annoyed the Marines at Khe Sanh. They felt they were on top of the enemy and had no need of being saved.

The siege of Khe Sanh officially lasted until April 5th. The Marines referred to it as '77 days of hell'. However, in reality, 7,000 N.V.A. remained roaming in the area and fighting continued until the summer. 703 Marines and A.R.V.N. had died during the siege. N.V.A. losses are estimated at anywhere between 10 -15,000.

By the time U.S. warplanes had ceased bombing missions in support of the Marines at Khe Sanh, it's estimated they dropped over 100,000 tons of bombs on the enemy. 158,000 artillery shells had been expended at N.V.A. positions. The area around Khe Sanh had become the most bombed area in the history of warfare.

With the siege 'won', and the spotlight shifted away from Khe Sanh, Johnson had the base quietly shut down and demolished on July 5th 1968. All personnel were withdrawn. Hanoi saw this as a victory and Hanoi Radio crowed about the fact for weeks, while Ho Chi Minh sent a personal message of congratulations to his troops in the area.

WHAT'S GOING ON ?

In the Spring of 1968, President Johnson had a lot more to contend with than just the fate of Khe Sanh. In America, 1968 was an election year. Johnson's presidency was up and if he wanted to stand for a second term of office, he had to decide very soon. Things didn't look good. One of his arch-rivals in the Democratic Party, Senator Eugene McCarthy, was seen to be very popular with

ABOVE LEFT: Soldiers take part in Operation "Tra Hung Doa," a search and destroy mission | **ABOVE RIGHT:** 3rd Marine Division during construction of a mountain-top fire support base

fellow Democrats – and an opinion poll revealed that Democratic loyalists were supporting him precisely because he wasn't Johnson. Johnson now had a personal approval rating of just 36% with the American people – and his policy in Vietnam was backed by just 26%. Johnson's weakness and unpopularity encouraged Robert Kennedy to stand for the Democratic presidential candidature too.

In the wake of Tet, Johnson was hearing all kinds of bad news about the war. Analyst David Shoup spoke out saying that the only way to win was to invade the North but Shoup would not recommend such a course of action. Defence Secretary Clifford was calling the war *'a real loser'*. In just six weeks, 'basic support' for the Vietnam War amongst the American people plunged from 74% to 54% - mostly due to Tet but also to Khe Sanh. In desperation, on the 25th March Johnson convened a panel of nine retired presidential advisors who were quickly given the nickname of 'The Wise Men'. The 'Wise Men' advised Johnson to stop pouring in troops and instead to try and find some sort of peace settlement. Johnson had expected advice on how to win the war – not how to bow out – and was livid.

On March 22nd, Johnson moved General Westmoreland to Army Chief of Staff and installed General Creighton Adams as commander of all U.S. Forces in Vietnam.

Johnson was now a very sick and frail man, broken by the responsibilities of the war. He knew by now that America could not win and that everything he had done or could do was futile. On March 31st, he went on television to announce the cessation of some U.S. bombing missions in the North. And then he dropped his bombshell: He would not be standing for re-election of President of the United States. He had had enough. Hanoi responded on April 3rd by calling the cessation of bombing 'a trick'. Johnson meekly said that he would try to establish talks with the North.

ABOVE LEFT: 3rd Marine Division set up two M-101 105mm howitzers during construction of a mountain-top fire support base | **ABOVE CENTRE:** Battle of Kham Duc. Company A, 70th Engineer Battalion, waiting to be airlifted out of Kham Duc | **TOP:** US Army tank traveling along Route 9 during Operation Pegasus

PEACE TALKS

It took nearly a month for the Americans and the North Vietnamese to even decide where to hold peace talks. At first Hanoi insisted on Warsaw but because Poland was behind the Iron Curtain that was unacceptable to the Americans. In the end, they agreed on Paris.

Talks started on May 10th 1968. South Vietnam was effectively excluded from discussions. They were not best pleased and tried to insist that talks should only be between the North and South regimes, even though the South would never recognise the communist party. The North Vietnamese delegation tried to use the talks to get the Americans to stop bombing in all areas north of the DMZ. The Americans refused unless N.V.A. troops were removed north of the DMZ. Then the North wanted Viet Cong guerrillas at the table. The U.S. said no very quickly and categorically. By June, the leader of South Vietnam was desperately trying to prevent the U.S. from making too many concessions, warning that the North would only see it as a sign of weakness. By July, the North were accusing the Americans of being *'infinitely obstinate'* and President Johnson was having to personally reassure the South Vietnamese President that his nation would not be sold out.

There would be no early – or easy – settlement.

WAR AND PEACE

As the diplomats talked and wined and dined in Paris, the war in Vietnam blazed on regardless. Indeed, they just made things worse. Both sides wanted to negotiate only from positions of strength – and that meant fighting even harder.

On April 30th, N.V.A. regulars had tried to invade South Vietnam through the DMZ. They were stopped by just a battalion of U.S. Marines later nicknamed 'the Magnificent Bastards' at the battle of Dai Do. In the five day engagement, 81 Marines were killed along with 29 Army soldiers acting in support. N.V.A. losses were estimated at 1,568 killed.

As Dai Do ended, The Viet Cong launched 'Tet II', attacking 120 cities throughout South Vietnam – including Saigon – with missiles and mortars. It's estimated that almost 6,000 Viet Cong guerrillas would die during the offensive. At the same time, up in Thua Thien Province, another 3,299 enemy combatants were reported dead as elements of the 101st Airborne took part in Operation Nevada Eagle and the 1st Air Cav in Quang Tri and Thua Thien claimed another 2,000 'kills'. 2,728 enemy dead were reported by the 1st Marine Division in Operation Marmaluke Thrust in Quang Nam. The communists were being hit hard, but it didn't stop them from attacking Saigon again on May 25th. During the fighting, the U.S. captured documents showing that the whole aim of the offensive was to put pressure on the Americans at the negotiating table in Paris. A fourth assault on Saigon, (planned for July 1968) was only stopped when A.R.V.N. and U.S. forces accidentally stumbled upon massive hidden Viet Cong arms caches.

Operation Pegasus: American soldiers aiding South Vietnamese forces to lift the siege of Khe Sanh.

ABOVE: SP4 Orman Osborn carrying M-60 machine gun across a stream

Mid-August saw Hanoi trying to put still greater pressure on the Americans, launching 15 different attacks on Tay Ninh and Binh Long provinces. The Capital of Tay Minh was only saved by American armour rushed to the scene. Within just two to three weeks, a combination of N.V.A. and Viet Cong tried to retake the city but ultimately failed.

That same month, the Democratic National Convention in Chicago sparked massive riots, but this time – according to many witnesses – it was the police who were doing the rioting. Whether pursuing demonstrators into Grant Park with chants of *'Kill! Kill! Kill! Kill!'* or beating people inside the Democratic Convention itself, it seemed for a time as if the police were totally out of control. America was coming apart.

NEGOTIATIONS GRIND ON

With a lack of any real progress in the Paris peace talks, an exasperated General Secretary U Thant stood before the U.N. on September 26th and suggested that North and South Vietnam should get together and sort their problems out. The Americans would effectively be excluded – and should stop their bombing for good measure.

On October 31st, President Johnson announced an end to Operation Rolling Thunder. There was to be no more bombing of North Vietnam. In turn, the North Vietnamese government conceded that the South Vietnamese could have a seat at the Paris table.

The problem was, South Vietnam didn't want one now. Within three days, President Thieu of South Vietnam was telling his assembly that Saigon would be boycotting the talks they had just been invited to. He thought the communists

Corp M.R. Carter guards an NVA soldier he captured during a ground movement ten miles northeast of An Hoa

ABOVE LEFT: A helicopter lowers an M101 105 mm howitzer into position | ABOVE RIGHT: Operation Tra Hung Doa Members of the 1st Plt, wearing protective masks, wait for orders to move out

were getting too much recognition while President Ky denounced President Johnson's decision to cancel Operation Rolling Thunder. *'We can no longer trust the Americans,'* he said. *'They are just a band of crooks.'* Four days later, Richard Milhous Nixon was elected the 37th President of the United States on a 'Peace With Honour' ticket.

South Vietnam changed their minds and decided to come to the negotiating table on 26th November. The talks then rapidly descended into a spiteful and protracted squabble about seating arrangements and who should have more status than whom. The negotiating parties couldn't even reach a working definition of who was actually waging war on whom.

THE TV WAR

Today, it's widely believed that the United States of America lost the Vietnam War in 1968. It just ran on for a few tortuous years while the whole bloody mess was cleaned up. In 1968, America won the Tet Offensive and caused the Viet Cong such devastating losses that it never recovered as a fighting force. It won the battle of Hue and it held magnificently at Khe Sanh. That year, it won every major battle and yet it lost the war. Its heart simply gave out. America

was the first television war and America simply couldn't stomach what it was seeing every night on its TV sets, even when it was winning. TV news brought the fear and tension of Khe Sanh, the exhausting street fighting in Hue and the large scale chaos of Tet and placed it just ten feet from the American eyeball. Respected news broadcasters became more cynical and questioning, anti-war demonstrations appeared more pervasive and representative of the American people than they really were and – with Johnson sick and near exhaustion – there was no one to rally the cause. If the politicians wouldn't speak up for the war, who would? *'Television is an instrument that can paralyze the country',* said General Westmoreland. *'Television brought the brutality of war into the comfort of the living room. Vietnam was lost in the living rooms of America--not on the battlefields of Vietnam,'* concluded media analyst Marshall McLuhan.

The debate still rages about how much a nation can tolerate the free reporting of war, especially when the opponent has full press control and effective means of censorship. The issue is likely to remain a vitally important one through the first half of the 21st century.

By the end of 1968, the number of U.S. personnel in Vietnam was at its height of 536,100.

1969

Meeting at Camp David to discuss the Vietnam situation

A SQUARE PEG

It was just one more of the dreadful ironies that plagued the Vietnam War that President Nixon successfully promoted himself into the White House on the 'Peace With Honour' ticket. Nixon was no admirer – and certainly no friend – of the Peace Movement, and would find more than a few choice names to call them over the next few years. He felt his natural constituency was 'Square America', men with short haircuts and ladies in sensible dresses who were, in his own words, *'the silent majority'*. Nixon was square and proud.

The War had done for Johnson, and Nixon thought he was made of sterner stuff. What's more he didn't care much about Vietnam. It was 'a sideshow'. All that mattered was how his policies on Vietnam played to the Soviets and the Chinese and to a lesser extent his Western Allies. Nixon had a global view, and Vietnam truly didn't matter in the grand scheme of things as long as it reflected positively on him and his nation.

PEACE THROUGH STRENGTH

When the peace talks resumed on January 2nd 1969, there was immediate deadlock. Delegates could not decide on the shape of their conference table. They finally settled on circular on January 16th, but then couldn't decide how many factions there were to sit around the table.

By the time Nixon had been inaugurated as president on January 20th and the peace talks looked like they might finally get moving meaningfully again in Paris, both sides were still fighting hard to be able to negotiate from a position of strength.

President Richard Nixon

ABOVE LEFT: The stress of war can be seen in this Vietnamese villager eyes | **ABOVE RIGHT:** A game of baseball in Ap Uu Thoung hamlet. Part of pacification operations

Operation Rice Farmer was well underway in the Mekong Delta, with A.V.R.N. and U.S. Infantry units flushing out and killing almost 2,000 Viet Cong. A huge A.R.V.N. effort up in Quyet Thang would last all year and result in almost 38,000 enemy dead by December 1969. U.S. Marines were hunting the enemy in the A Shau Valley in Quang Tri Province.

On the communist side, the Viet Cong had mortared several towns and military bases, attacked a supply convoy North West of Saigon and assassinated the South Vietnamese Education Minister. In late February 1969, they launched attacks on 117 South Vietnamese towns and cities including Saigon, and succeeded in killing 36 U.S. Marines in a single strike by a suicide squad up near the DMZ. A total of 435 U.S. personnel had been killed in what became known as the 'Post Tet' Offensive, leading American diplomats to hint heavily that U.S. bombing raids on the north could be resumed again in response to the flaring guerrilla war. Hanoi responded by simply stepping up the violence, probably testing the resolve of newly elected President Nixon.

Nixon responded with strength. On March 15th he sent U.S. Marines into the DMZ and three days later used B-52s to bomb communist camps actually inside supposedly neutral Cambodia. Operation Breakfast, as it was called, was kept secret from the public. More than 3,600 bombing sorties were flown over Cambodia over the next fourteen months, dropping 111,000 bombs. The bombing of Cambodia stayed secret for just two months. In May 1969, the New York Times revealed the secret bombing campaign to the world. The American public – Nixon's 'square constituency' cared very little in response. The reaction of the Peace Movement – and many world leaders - was a good deal more hostile.

HEARTS AND MINDS

'99% of the people hoped that the war would go away and leave them alone'
Edward Lansdale, America's First Intelligence Chief in Vietnam.

Sometimes President Johnson called it 'Hearts and Minds'. Sometimes he called it 'Minds and Hearts'. Officially, the strategy to win over the Vietnam peasant villager was called 'Pacification'. It was a good idea - in theory. Under Pacification, the rural population – 85% of all South Vietnamese – would get new schools and clinics, roads and water supplies, better food, and increased safety and security. The idea had been present in some form or another in Vietnam for years. There was just one problem. It didn't work.

For one thing, the Viet Cong were too strongly entrenched in the villages. They had killed over 37,000 villagers who had disobeyed or displeased them and they were powerful and feared. If the Saigon regime sent a new teacher to a village, they'd just kill her. A new well would be blown up. The Americans, supposedly the great benefactors, would often terrorise villages as much as the V.C. had ever done, especially during Search & Destroy operations. The Americans, it seemed to the average villager, were utterly baffling foreigners who gave with one hand and killed with the other.

After Tet had devastated the Viet Cong in the villages, Hearts and Minds did pick up pace and really started to achieve something in a safer and calmer time. But then Operation Phoenix helped to unravel it all again.

PHOENIX

They called it Operation Phoenix because they couldn't think of another name. By 1969, U.S. intelligence realised just how devastating Tet had been to the V.C. and decided to go after what remained of them – hard. Operation Phoenix was a CIA-led initiative designed to get into South Vietnamese villages and destroy what was left of the communist guerrilla force. The special forces used were officially called PRU teams but they soon became known as 'Hit Teams' instead. They bribed, they tortured and they killed and they killed – sometimes entirely the wrong people. Their village raids often resembled in violence and terror just what the Viet Cong had themselves done a decade earlier. Hearts were enraged. Minds turned to revenge. Operation Phoenix ran until 1971 during which time 28,000 suspected Viet Cong were captured and 'interrogated' and another 20,000 killed. It undoubtedly had a real effect of the V.C. structures in the villages but equally undoubtedly alienated and brutalised the very people they were trying to free. It was almost a metaphor for the greater war effort.

HAMBURGER HILL

The locals called the heavily forested, 3,000 feet high peak Ap Bia Mountain. The U.S. Military officially designated it Hill 937 – but to the men of the 101st Airborne charged with taking it in May 1969, the place would always be known as 'Hamburger Hill'.

The battle for Hamburger Hill was part of Operation Apache Snow, an attempt

TOP: Original unissued patch for the Phoenix Program | **LEFT:** Sergeant Curtis Hester firing his M-16 rifle while Sergeant Billy Faulks calls for air support

A Vietnamese civilian with a gun pointed at the side of her head.

to stop N.V.A. units sneaking out of Laos and menacing Hue and Da Nang. The Hill was crowned by a heavily fortified N.V.A. stronghold. For days it was blitzed by air strikes and artillery bombardments while men of the 101st tried to storm its steep muddy slopes with no success. It was only on their 11th attempt that they managed to breach and overrun the N.V.A. base. 56 paratroopers died and a further 420 were wounded.

Having fought so long and so hard to take Hamburger Hill, the men of the 101st were dismayed in the least when their C.O. ordered them off of the hill and on to another objective. Within a few days the N.V.A. had returned to Hamburger Hill and were back in their old positions once more.

When the story broke in the American media, Congress was outraged. One senator called the action 'senseless and irresponsible'. General Abrams was now instructed to launch no more large-scale Search & Destroy missions and to concentrate on much smaller actions instead.

THE NIXON DOCTRINE

Richard Nixon was never the most patient or hands-off kind of man. The Paris Peace Talks were going nowhere – and not even going nowhere fast. They were going nowhere at a snail's pace.

Even as the men of the 101st Airborne were scrambling and dying assaulting the slopes of Hamburger Hill, Nixon was appearing on TV presenting a new peace plan. He suggested both the Americans and North Vietnamese pulled out of the South completely over the next year. Hanoi showed no interest. Now Nixon moved on to a meeting with South Vietnam's President Nguyen Van Thieu where he laid down the law. U.S. combat troops would start to withdraw in significant numbers, he told Thieu. The war would be 'Vietnamised' and the South expected to do more and more of its own fighting.

ABOVE LEFT: Members of Companies B and D, 1st Battalion, 501st Infantry, Regiment, 101st Airborne Division, take a break from jungle fighting east of Tam Ky
ABOVE CENTRE: Company M, 3d Battalion, 3d Marines smoke a cigarette on patrol below Mutter's Ridge | **ABOVE RIGHT:** Soldiers carry a wounded comrade through a swamp

Men of Troop B, 1st Battalion, 10th Cavalry Regiment, 4th Infantry Division move through the jungle in the Central Highlands of Vietnam in a M-48 Patton tank

1970

President Nixon points out the NVA sanctuaries along the Cambodian border

VIETNAM IN 1970

In Paris, the talks were hopelessly deadlocked. In Vietnam, both sides fought on. January 1970 saw massive B-52 strikes against the Ho Chi Minh Trail in the hope of cutting off resupply to the Viet Cong and reducing N.V.A. units invading the South. It didn't work. Viet Cong raids in the South were on the increase. On January 16th, the Viet Cong attacked a civilian refugee camp at Chauthan and slaughtered 16 civilians by throwing sticks of dynamite into their houses. In March, the Viet Cong bombed a Buddhist temple at Hoc Man, killing 14 women and children. Another attack on a Buddhist orphanage and temple, on August 29th, killed 14 children. On May 6th, 450 civilians were murdered by Viet Cong raids in just one week – a grim record. Throughout the year, the Viet Cong claimed to have killed 6,000 civilians believed to have been collaborating with the Saigon Government.

The ground war went on unabated throughout the country. Numerous Americans were killed in surprise mortar attacks on bases or in ambushes out in the field. Corresponding counter attacks left hundreds if not thousands of V.C. and N.V.A. dead after the incidents. Nixon began to make ominous warnings if that Hanoi didn't reign in its attacks, there would be a heavy price to pay. He was, after all, completely 'Boo Coo Dinky Dau'.

In August, B-52s were hammering N.V.A. positions throughout the DMZ and by December, President Nixon was warning Hanoi that the North would once again receive the same treatment if Viet Cong activity wasn't curtailed – and fast.

Bayonne temple, Angkor Thom, Siem Reap, Cambodia

PEACE TALKS

It took nearly a month for the Americans and the North Vietnamese to even decide where to hold peace talks. At first Hanoi insisted on Warsaw but because Poland was behind the Iron Curtain that was unacceptable to the Americans. In the end, they agreed on Paris.

Talks started on May 10th 1968. South Vietnam was effectively excluded from discussions. They were not best pleased and tried to insist that talks should only be between the North and South regimes, even though the South would never recognise the communist party. The North Vietnamese delegation tried to use the talks to get the Americans to stop bombing in all areas north of the DMZ. The Americans refused unless N.V.A. troops were removed north of the DMZ. Then the North wanted Viet Cong guerrillas at the table. The U.S. said no very quickly and categorically. By June, the leader of South Vietnam was desperately trying to prevent the U.S. from making too many concessions, warning that the North would only see it as a sign of weakness. By July, the North were accusing the Americans of being 'infinitely obstinate' and President Johnson was having to personally reassure the South Vietnamese President that his nation would not be sold out.

There would be no early – or easy – settlement.

WAR AND PEACE

As the diplomats talked and wined and dined in Paris, the war in Vietnam blazed on regardless. Indeed, they just made things worse. Both sides wanted to negotiate only from positions of strength – and that meant fighting even harder.

On April 30th, N.V.A. regulars had tried to invade South Vietnam through the DMZ. They were stopped by just a battalion of U.S. Marines later nicknamed 'the Magnificent Bastards' at the battle of Dai Do. In the five day engagement, 81 Marines were killed along with 29 Army soldiers acting in support. N.V.A. losses were estimated at 1,568 killed.

As Dai Do ended, The Viet Cong launched 'Tet II', attacking 120 cities throughout South Vietnam – including Saigon – with missiles and mortars. It's estimated that almost 6,000 Viet Cong guerrillas would die during the offensive. At the same time, up in Thua Thien Province, another 3,299 enemy combatants were reported dead as elements of the 101st Airborne took part in Operation Nevada Eagle and the 1st Air Cav in Quang Tri and Thua Thien claimed another 2,000 'kills'. 2,728 enemy dead were reported by the 1st Marine Division in Operation Marmaluke Thrust in Quang Nam. The communists were being hit hard, but it didn't stop them from attacking Saigon again on May 25th. During the fighting, the U.S. captured documents showing that the whole aim of the offensive was to put pressure on the Americans at the negotiating table in Paris. A fourth assault on Saigon, (planned for July 1968) was only stopped when A.R.V.N. and U.S. forces accidentally stumbled upon massive hidden Viet Cong arms caches.

Operation Pegasus: American soldiers aiding South Vietnamese forces to lift the siege of Khe Sanh.

In July 1969, Nixon then sent secret communiques to Ho Chi Minh himself via a French contact, pressuring him to settle the war and strongly hinting that U.S. Bombing of the North would resume if he didn't. Ho eventually responded with a tirade of abuse against the 'American Aggressors' and said that he supported Hanoi's position. Ho was actually gravely sick by now and removed from day to day events. On September 2nd, Ho Chi Minh died, aged 79. He was killed by a heart attack brought about by his diabetes.

As Nixon was drafting his message to Ho Chi Minh, 800 men of the 9th Infantry Division became the first American unit in Vietnam to be withdrawn and sent home by the President. The plan was for a 14 stage withdrawal that would finally see all US troops out of Vietnam by November 1972. The war would now be fought by what became known as the 'Nixon Doctrine'. America would provide economic and military aid to nations fighting communism – and it would further support those nations with air power – but there would be no more American boys doing what South East Asian boys should be doing for themselves.

Meanwhile, in typical Nixon administration fashion, National Security Advisor Henry Kissinger was arranging top secret talks with contacts in Hanoi behind the backs of his South Vietnamese Allies. Let the official peace talks chatter on. The real powers were going to sort things out themselves. Kissinger's tactic was to tell his North Vietnamese counterpart that Nixon was '*Boo Coo Dinky Dau*' – much crazy in the head. Playing 'Good Cop' to Nixon's 'Bad Cop', Kissinger warned the Vietnamese that Nixon was capable of anything and that they had better negotiate. Whenever he needed a demonstration that Nixon was Dinky Dau, Kissinger would have a friendly word with the President to ramp up some bombing.

In October, it was revealed that 71% of Americans now approved of the Nixon Doctrine – but those who didn't kept on demonstrating, much to Hanoi's delight. North Vietnam's Prime Minister Pham Van Dong sent a personal letter to the leaders of the anti-war movement which was read out to the demonstrators at the Moratorium Rallies held in Washington and several other major U.S. Cities.

The notion of the enemy leader virtually addressing 'Peaceniks' on American soil infuriated the Nixon administration. Vice President Spiro Agnew led the attacks, calling the demonstrators communist 'dupes' and describing them as '*an effete corps of impudent snobs who characterize themselves as intellectuals.*' Nixon went on TV and warned that division in America would only encourage the North not to negotiate. The anti-war movement responded with the 'Mobilization' peace demonstration – the largest anti-war rally in American history, which drew over a quarter of a million protestors to Washington D.C. on November 15th 1969.

There were now 474,000 U.S. service personnel in Vietnam, sixty thousand fewer than the year before.

Capt. Larry Buts on air boat patrol in the Mekong Delta with Chinese Merceneries and American advisers

1970

President Nixon points out the NVA sanctuaries along the Cambodian border

VIETNAM IN 1970

In Paris, the talks were hopelessly deadlocked. In Vietnam, both sides fought on. January 1970 saw massive B-52 strikes against the Ho Chi Minh Trail in the hope of cutting off resupply to the Viet Cong and reducing N.V.A. units invading the South. It didn't work. Viet Cong raids in the South were on the increase. On January 16th, the Viet Cong attacked a civilian refugee camp at Chauthan and slaughtered 16 civilians by throwing sticks of dynamite into their houses. In March, the Viet Cong bombed a Buddhist temple at Hoc Man, killing 14 women and children. Another attack on a Buddhist orphanage and temple, on August 29th, killed 14 children. On May 6th, 450 civilians were murdered by Viet Cong raids in just one week – a grim record. Throughout the year, the Viet Cong claimed to have killed 6,000 civilians believed to have been collaborating with the Saigon Government.

The ground war went on unabated throughout the country. Numerous Americans were killed in surprise mortar attacks on bases or in ambushes out in the field. Corresponding counter attacks left hundreds if not thousands of V.C. and N.V.A. dead after the incidents. Nixon began to make ominous warnings if that Hanoi didn't reign in its attacks, there would be a heavy price to pay. He was, after all, completely *'Boo Coo Dinky Dau'*.

In August, B-52s were hammering N.V.A. positions throughout the DMZ and by December, President Nixon was warning Hanoi that the North would once again receive the same treatment if Viet Cong activity wasn't curtailed – and fast.

Bayonne temple, Angkor Thom, Siem Reap, Cambodia

Boeing B-52D-35-BW Stratofortress dropping bombs over Vietnam

CAMBODIA

On March 18th 1970, something happened that changed everything. Ruling Prince Sihanouk of Cambodia was deposed by his military, led by General Lon Nol. Determined not to go down without a fight, Prince Sihanouk then formed an alliance with his country's communist underground – the Khmer Rouge, who were led by a then completely unknown zealot named Pol Pot.

General Lon Nol quickly went on the offensive, attacking not only the Khmer Rouge guerrillas but also North Vietnamese forces inside Cambodia. The Cambodian military's efforts did not go well though, and they were soon in a vulnerable position. The White House tried to react as quickly as possible to support their newfound ally and pumped $500 million in aid to the new military regime in just two weeks. Then, at the end of April 1970, President Nixon announced that U.S. and South Vietnamese forces would be going into Cambodia in support of the Cambodian military. Just two days after the coup, American artillery was firing over the border in support of Cambodian army units fighting the Viet Cong. By the end of March, U.S. helicopter gunships were strafing Viet Cong positions in support of South Vietnamese units moving into Cambodia.

The anti-war movement in America exploded with fury. Nixon had promised an American withdrawal from Vietnam but now he was actively expanding the conflict in the region and getting involved in an entirely new war, at least in the eyes of the protestors.

Events were equally ominous in Cambodia. The N.V.A. were proving themselves an exceptionally tough opponent for General Lon Nol's rather weak army and were now driving in force towards Cambodia's capital Phnom

Navy inshore patrol craft, PCF-38 of Coastal Division 11, Cai Ngay Canal

Penh. American air strikes hammered at them around the clock to stop their progress.

May 1st is a traditional communist holiday worldwide. That's why it was chosen for the day on which 15,000 U.S. and 5,000 A.R.V.N. troops surged into Cambodia, concentrating their efforts against the N.V.A. supply bases that had long been off limits due to international niceties. For their part, the N.V.A. largely melted away and avoided any full scale fight, but their abandoned bases were destroyed and valuable weapons and supply caches lost.

As U.S. soldiers manoeuvred on Cambodian soil, back home President Nixon lost his temper with demonstrators and called them 'bums'. In reaction, the next day there were violent and chaotic demonstrations on university campuses all over America. Things came to a head with terrifying speed. On May 4th, four unarmed protestors - two of them women - were shot dead by elements of the National Guard at Kent State University in Ohio. Nine more were shot and wounded. It was a sobering moment for the Nixon administration. Armed troops had just shot dead students in America. A grieving parent of one of the dead students was interviewed on television, snarling, 'My child was not a bum!' The anti-war movement merely stepped up their efforts. Over 400 colleges and universities were immediately shut down in protest over the student killings and more than 100,000 demonstrators swarmed into Washington D.C. to protest. On May 8th, pro-war American construction workers descended on an anti-war demonstration of Wall Street and beat up 70 protestors. Twelve days later, New York saw a march by over 100,000 New Yorkers in support of President Nixon's policies.

Nixon decided to stay firm. The Squares were behind him. On June 3rd, he announced that the U.S. incursion into Cambodia had been 'the most successful operation of this long and difficult war' and said that American troop withdrawals from Vietnam could now be resumed. All American combat troops returned from

ABOVE: Sergeant Robert Fears clears an area using his flamethrower. Da Nang
LEFT: An exhausted American infantryman lies amongst his fellow soldiers, Fishhook area, Cambodia/Vietnam frontier

Photograher David Hume Kennerly photographs a helicopter from a hot landing zone in the Central Highlands of Vietnam

Cambodia on June 30th, having suffered 354 soldiers killed in action during the incursion. Bombing missions in Cambodia would remain numerous and vigorous. South Vietnamese troops would launch a new offensive inside Cambodia in October under a separate accord agreed between the South Vietnamese and Lon Nol, but by December 1970, American commanders were forbidden to join in. An emergency amendment to the U.S. defence appropriations bill refused to fund any U.S. ground forces fighting in either Laos or Cambodia.

CHAOS IN THE RANKS

There was now a major crisis growing within the U.S. military in Vietnam. Search & Destroy was very largely a thing of the past and no one really knew what to do with the troops still in country. They were just there. There were patrols, but with little purpose and at considerable risk. Everyone knew they would be coming home soon. The Peace Talks were on and no one wanted to be the last man to die in a war that was all over except for the shooting.

At the same time, the calibre of new draftees being brought in to serve was considerably different. They were young. The average age of an infantryman in Vietnam was nineteen. In World War Two it was twenty six. One officer consequently described his men as 'immature' and 'very emotional'. Racial tensions reached new heights. Blacks were statistically more likely to be assigned combat duty rather than safer 'Rear Echelon' assignments – and they knew it. Simmering hatreds from the Civil Rights movement were brought to fresh life thousands of miles from the streets of Mobile. Many new draftees had been with the Peace Movement before being called up or had been living alternative lifestyles. Mom's apple pie meant less to them than bitchin' reefer.

By 1971, an official report estimated that around 15% of all U.S. soldiers in Vietnam were taking hallucinogens and 22% were heroin addicts. That same year, while 5,000 soldiers were treated for combat injuries, over 20,000 needed to be treated for drug-related abuse.

Officers struggled to retain some level of control. Between 1969 and 1971 the U.S. Army's desertion rate quadrupled, not just in Vietnam but on bases throughout the world. In 1970, there were no less than 35 individual 'combat refusals' – or mutinies – in the 1st Air Cavalry alone. A new word entered the troops' vocabulary – 'Fragging'. Fragging was the murder of an officer who gave orders that put you into danger or – if you were really P.O'd that day – you just didn't like or looked at you funny. Maybe he was just a 'Number Ten Honky'. Fragging got its name because many attacks on officers were carried out using fragmentation grenades, perhaps rolled into their tent while they were off duty. Between 1969 and 1971, 730 fragging incidents were officially reported, with 83 American officers killed as a direct result. This report only included incidents using grenades. Attacks on U.S. officers by their own men using guns and knives were over and above that figure.

The chaos and disillusionment spread all the way up the chain of command. Field officers were becoming very mindful of fragging and so became more and more cautious. Most would only ever serve six months in Vietnam before pursuing their careers elsewhere. They just wanted to get it over and come out in one piece. At the very top, the most senior officers thought that the politicians had sold them out – along with a significant slice of the very people they were fighting for. Despite being asked to fight with one (or more) arms tied behind their backs, they had delivered considerable military success – only to have the politicians talk it all away over lunch or dinner.

At the end of 1970 there were 335,800 U.S. personnel still in Vietnam. It was way past time to go home.

ABOVE LEFT: Navy SEALS X-Ray Platoon. Taken on a dock near Ben Tre in Southeast Vietnam | ABOVE RIGHT: WAC class on pack closing the T-10 Parachute at the 90th Aerial Equipment Depot, Saigon | OPPOSITE PAGE: Young South Vietnamese men, who will return to their villages after 13 weeks' at the National Training Center, to help villagers help themselves

1971

Henry A. Kissinger

Specialist. 4 Richard Champion, squad leader, shouts instructions to his squad while receiving sniper fire on Hill 56

'THE END IS IN SIGHT'

On January 4th 1971, President Nixon announced that – as far as the Vietnam War was concerned 'The end is in sight'.

What gave rise to this sudden bout of optimism isn't known. The Paris Peace Talks were going nowhere and even Kissinger's secret talks with the enemy behind South Vietnam's back were achieving nothing. Nixon's own men were soon keen to disabuse him of the notion of any blue skies immediately ahead. 'There are some rough days ahead,' warned Defence Secretary Melvin Laird, while Chairman of the US Joint Chiefs of Staff Admiral Thomas Moorer concluded that the situation in Cambodia was 'deteriorating'.

THE CAMBODIAN CRISIS

Even as Nixon's advisors struggled to tell the President not to be complacent, U.S. aircraft were launching fresh heavy strikes against N.V.A. camps in both Cambodia and Laos.

At the end of January 1971, the South Vietnamese launched Operation Lam Son 719, sending 17,000 A.R.V.N. troops into Laos to sever the Ho Chi Minh Trail. Nixon pointed to this as proof of the success of his 'Vietnamisation' policy. Here were the South Vietnamese fighting for themselves, by themselves. It wasn't true of course. The A.R.V.N. forces were airlifted in by U.S. helicopters and received critical artillery and air support from the U.S. as well. Instead of proving that the South Vietnamese could stand on their own two feet, Operation Lam Son 719 simply revealed that they couldn't.

Early April saw Lam Son 719 end in abject failure, as the survivors of the A.R.V.N. units who had gone into Laos fled back across the border hotly pursued by 40,000 N.V.A.

ABOVE LEFT: ACAV's of South Vietnamese 1st Armored Brigade on Route 9 in Laos
ABOVE RIGHT: The "bomb farm" onboard the aircraft carrier USS Kitty Hawk

troops. Every airworthy helicopter transport in the U.S. fleet had to be mobilised to help rescue them. Fully half of the soldiers they had sent in had been killed. 2315 American support personnel had also been killed, and the U.S. had lost over 100 helicopters and had another 600 damaged. Despite this, the powers-that-be in Saigon still held a victory parade.

LOSING FAITH

Spring 1971 saw no let-up in the protest against the Vietnam War. By March, Nixon's conduct of the war was approved of by just 34% of the population – and fully half of America now agreed that the war was 'morally wrong'. March saw the Capitol building in Washington D.C. bombed and damaged by violent anti-war radicals. In mid-April, 'Vietnam Veterans Against the War' spearheaded a week of protests across America while on April 24th, almost 200,000 protestors swarmed into Washington D.C.

COMING HOME

The last U.S. Marine combat forces left Vietnam, on April 30th 1970. It was a milestone of a sort. The previous day had seen another milestone – the death of the forty nine thousandth U.S. serviceman in Vietnam. In mid-August both Australia and New Zealand announced that they intended to withdraw all of their personnel from the theatre too.

Nixon had pursued vigorous troop withdrawals throughout the year and by the end of 1971 there were significantly fewer U.S. service personnel in country – 159,000

Navy McDonnell F-4B Phantom II drops 227 kg Mk 82 bombs over Vietnam

Tan Son Nhut Air Base, Sergeant Richard L. Moser signals to start the engine of a U.S. Air Force RB-57 prior to a mission

Anti-war protest against the Vietnam War in Washington, D.C. on April 24th 1971

U.S. Marines from the 5th Regiment say goodbye to Vietnam as they board the LPH-9, USS Denver

1972

USS Henry W Tucker off_Vietnam 1972

MORE TALK

In January 1972, Nixon offered up an eight point plan for peace. He also revealed that Kissinger had been in secret talks with the Hanoi regime behind South Vietnam's back.

In late February, Nixon shocked the world by visiting communist China. Here, he and Kissinger met with Mao-Tse-Tung and his Prime Minister. Again, Kissinger secretly warned the communists that he was afraid of Nixon, that his boss was crazy and sometimes almost desperate to press the big red button.

The meeting between Mao and Nixon shook the Hanoi regime. Better relations between the two superpowers might mean a weakening of China's commitment to their cause. Certainly Nixon felt confident enough in March 1972 to announce he was going to boycott the Paris Peace Talks because the communists were not 'negotiating seriously'. The talks broke down once more.

THE EASTERTIDE OFFENSIVE

Unsure now of China's long term commitment to their cause, the Hanoi regime decided on a wild gamble. They would invade South Vietnam.

While their Viet Cong compatriot forces had been almost wiped out by the disastrous Tet campaign of 1968, they still had many N.V.A. infiltrators behind enemy lines. As the American Hawks - and the South Vietnamese government -

Mao-Tse-Tung

Aerial view of bombing raid during Operation Linebacker I

had warned the North had taken America's troops withdrawals as a sign of weakness and lack of commitment to helping South Vietnam stay free. They were also thoroughly heartened by the anti-war movement in America, and – this being an election year – thought that Nixon would be too scared of losing the election to fight back properly. They had no fear of the A.R.V.N.. They had proved themselves poor opponents in Operation Lam Son 719 the year before.

So, on March 30th 1972, the legendary General Giap led 200,000 N.V.A. troops south to settle the Vietnam War once and for all, in what became known as the Eastertide Offensive. His initial targets were Quang Tri, then Kontum and then An Loc.

Nixon responded hard. By April 2nd, the big guns and air power of the U.S. 7th Fleet were blazing away at troop concentrations in the DMZ. Two days later, he authorised a huge bombing campaign, hitting out both at N.V.A. troops invading South Vietnam and targets north of the DMZ. . He told his close advisors:

'The bastards have never been bombed like they're going to bombed this time,'

Four days later the B-52s were in the air, carpet bombing targets almost 150 miles inside the North. Targets around Hanoi and Haiphong Harbour were hit on April 15th. Still, the N.V.A. in the South rolled on and seemed unstoppable. A.R.V.N. forces fled Quang Tri on May 1st, leaving it to its fate. In Paris, the peace talks had resumed on April 27th but had collapsed again by May 4th, with America and South Vietnam declaring that talks were postponed indefinitely.

RIGHT: A wounded soldier lies near death alongside Highway 13 in Lai Khe

ABOVE: A McDonnell F-4J-34-MC Phantom II from Fighter Squadron VF-143 Pukin´ Dogs launching from USS Enterprise

OPERATION LINEBACKER

If the Hanoi regime had hoped that Nixon would race more troops back to Vietnam and thereby lose his chance of winning the presidential election, they were wrong. By now, there were only 10,000 U.S. troops left in Vietnam and they were scheduled to leave shortly but the decision was taken not to reinforce them. The South Vietnamese would bear the brunt of stopping the N.V.A.'s Eastertide Offensive on the ground, while U.S. Air Power would help to smash it from the skies.

Operation Pocket Money was launched from the aircraft carrier USS Coral Sea on May 8th. Six A-7 Corsair IIs and three A-6 Intruders dropped mines into Haiphong Harbor. The operation continued for another three days, with a total of some 11,000 mines being dropped into other North Vietnamese ports. By taking out its harbours, America had effectively deprived the north of 85% of all its imports. Now it went after the remaining 15%.

Operation Linebacker was intended to decimate North Vietnam's major roads, railways and rolling stock as well as its storage warehouses. It was also intended to tear apart the country's air defence system.

414 U.S.A.F. and U.S. Navy fighters and fighter-bombers flew combat sorties over the North on May 10th. – and the North Vietnamese Air Force came up to meet them. Dogfights raged all across the country, resulting in two F-4 Phantoms being shot down by enemy fighters and two Navy planes brought down by SAMs or anti-aircraft guns. The North Vietnamese Air Force lost four MiG-21s and seven MiG-17s.

By the end of May 1972, American commanders decided they had done enough damage to the transport infrastructure and switched to raids

U.S. Navy LTV A-7E Corsair II from Attack Squadron VA-27 Royal Maces launching from USS Enterprise

principally against oil storage facilities and enemy airfields. The dogfighting continued, with the U.S. Navy pilots achieving a ferocious 6:1 kill ration. It was claimed that communist pilots actively sought to avoid them. U.S.A.F. fighter pilots fared less well, and during the early months of Linebacker their kill ratio was 1:1 primarily because of outdated tactics. U.S.A.F. learned fast though, and by August 1972, their fighter pilots were achieving a more creditable 4:1 kill ratio.

EASTERTIDE FALTERS

The effect of the bombing on the N.V.A. forces invading South Vietnam was felt almost immediately. Only 30% of the supplies needed at the front line were now reaching communist units and there were desperate orders given to preserve ammunition. Shelling by the N.V.A. was cut by almost 50% in just a month.

On May 30th, Giap's attack on Kontum was beaten off with heavy losses. It was thwarted by a combination of determined A.R.V.N. ground forces and massive U.S. air strikes. A month later, South Vietnamese forces were fighting to retake Quang Tri Province in the North, again aided by U.S. air power and the big guns of U.S. Navy ships sitting offshore. Two weeks later, Giap's third and final assault, on An Loc in the South, was smashed by A.R.V.N. troops and carpet bombing by U.S.A.F. B-52 heavy bombers. The drive to free Bin Dinh Province started on July 18th and Quang Tri City finally fell to the South on September 16th. U.S. Air Raids on North Vietnamese airfields destroyed 10% of its entire air force on the night of September 29th.

It's estimated that the N.V.A. suffered 100,000 casualties in the Eastertide Offensive, as well as losing fully half the tanks and artillery committed to the campaign. No longer the People's Hero, General Giap was pushed aside in favour of General Dung (pronounced Zung).

Hanoi realised it had lost this round of the war. In late May 1972, President Nixon had travelled to Moscow to help thaw relations between America and the Soviet Union. As a result, while North Vietnam was being pulverised by Operation Linebacker, the communist superpowers had condemned American aggression but done nothing more. They wanted a better relationship and increased trade with America more than they wanted victory for some tin pot South East Asian paddy field.

Hanoi's only competing secret weapon in the conflict was Jane Fonda, who had spent a day in Hanoi in July posing for photos and making anti-American propaganda broadcasts on Hanoi Radio. Lovely as she was, it was not a fair fight.

By August, talks between Kissinger and his communist counterpart were on again.

LINEBACKER ENDS

Operation Linebacker finally ended on October 22nd. Over 40,000 combat sorties had been flown during the operation with over 125,000 tons of bombs

Sikorsky HH-53 Super Jolly Green Giant helicopter of the 40th Aerospace Rescue and Recovery Squadron, seen from the flight engineer's position a helicopter of the 21st Special Operations Squadron

128

being dropped on Vietnam. For the first time America had used considerable amounts of new laser guided and'smart' bombs, making their raids more effective and devastating than ever before. It was a salutary lesson for the North Vietnamese.

LAND GRAB

In October 1972, Kissinger made a massive concession to Hanoi at the Paris Peace Talks. He agreed that North Vietnamese troops could stay where they were in Vietnam after the Eastertide Offensive if the two halves of the country agreed to a ceasefire. Behind the scenes, Kissinger told President Thieu to *'seize as much territory as possible'* before the ceasefire was agreed. To help him do this, he arranged $2 billion worth of supplies, transferred U.S. bases scheduled for demolition to the A.R.V.N. and gave the South possession of lots of spare American kit. By November 1971, South Vietnam was in possession of the world's fourth largest air force. Some saw it as 'Vietnamisation'. Some saw it as bribery. Richard Nixon had good reason to feel generous though. On November 7th he had been re-elected to the White House with nothing less than the biggest landslide vote in American history.

Thieu was still not happy at the prospect of N.V.A. forces remaining in his country. Nixon tried to slap him down by threatening the end to all aid but Thieu held firm, coming up with complex and difficult counter-proposals. Any progress in the Peace Talks soon disappeared. No one trusted anyone else. Terms and conditions once agreed were changed in new draft proposals. The talks finally collapsed altogether on December 14th.

LINEBACKER II

President Nixon had set his heart on a ceasefire being in place by January 1973. Now the North Vietnamese had all but packed up and walked away from the table in Paris. It was time, Nixon decided, to get Boo Coo Dinky Dau on them big time. He issued a warning of *'grave consequences'* if Hanoi did not return to the negotiating table within 72 hours. They did not. Nixon now launched Operation Linebacker II, a three night intensive bombing of the North.

Night One saw 129 bombers sent against North Vietnamese air fields and targets around Hanoi, supported by 39 other support aircraft including F-4 Phantom fighter escorts and F-105 'Wild Weasel' SAM suppressors. 68 SAMs were launched against the bomber waves and three B-52s were shot down. Night Two saw 93 bombers with their support aircraft attack a power plant and railway installations without loss. Night three was very different. The North Vietnamese now had a much better grasp of U.S.A.F. bombing tactics and were well prepared when 99 bombers returned to attack railroad yards, power plants and other targets on the night of the 20th December. 34 SAMs were unleashed, with much greater effect. Eight B-52s were lost in a single night.

Nixon was told these losses were unacceptable. The Air Force blamed poor electronic counter measure systems on board the older B-52s. Nixon decided

Soldiers of 5th Airborne Brigade during attack by NVA heavy small-arms fire, along Highway 13, south of An Loc

to extend the bombing raids past the original 3 days – but to use only bombers with the best ECM equipment which meant smaller attacks in future. Despite this, the raids on the night of December 21st saw two more B-52s lost to SAMs but on the following night, when the attacks switched away to targets other than Hanoi, there were no losses. On the 22nd, a Hanoi hospital on the very edge of a military airfield was accidentally hit – and the world's press flooded in to witness the 'atrocity'. On the 23rd and 24th, no losses were experienced by the Americans, who also discovered that their F-111 Aardvarks could do a better job of supressing SAM sites than their Thunderchiefs.

The last strikes came on Christmas Eve 1972, when a 36 hour halt was called to the bombing to assess the situation. The commanders decided to shake up their tactics and go back in – harder than ever. Boxing Day evening saw 120 bombers and 113 support aircraft swarm over the North, overwhelming Hanoi's air defences. Two B-52s were lost to the North's rapidly dwindling supply of SAMs. The next night 60 bombers struck, with the loss of two B-52s and two F-4 Phantom fighter escorts. The same number of bombers returned the following night, with four of the six waves concentrated around Hanoi. No losses were reported.

By December 29th, U.S.A.F. commanders concluded that there was little of strategic value left in North Vietnam that was worth the effort to bomb. Still they went, targeting two SAM storage facilities without loss.

Public reaction was largely hostile. The Soviet Union and China protested of course, but it was Sweden's prime minister who shocked everyone by comparing the bombing raids to Guernica and the Holocaust. The U.S. responded by withdrawing their ambassador from Sweden and telling the country not to bother to send them an ambassador in future. In America, the anti-war movement denounced Nixon as 'a madman'.

But the North returned to the Paris negotiating table in short order. It was only South Vietnam's President Thieu who still had serious objections to the terms on the table. Nixon quickly shut him up by saying that, if he didn't fall in line, he might meet the same fate as President Diem.

America and South Vietnam were no longer friends.

GOING HOME

Somewhere in all the chaos of 1972 – the intensive bombing, the massed invasion of the south, the unparalleled superpower diplomacy, the Nixon landslide and the staccato peace talks – it's all-too-easy to overlook the biggest single event of the year.

1972 was the year when the last American combat soldier left South Vietnam. On March 10th, the 101st Airborne had said goodbye to the Nam for the final time. By April 30th there were less than 70,000 U.S. troops in the country and the very last combat troops left for home on August 23rd, 1972. An American president had kept his promise to his people.

And that president was Richard Milhous Nixon. (Of course on June 17th, 1972, five burglars were caught planting microphones in the Democratic National Committee offices, in the Watergate Hotel. But that's another story).

A refugee girl escapes the fighting as U.S. military tanks drive on the road near Lai Khe

1973

Paris peace talks Vietnam peace agreement signing

PEACE WITH HONOUR

By the second week of January 1973, both America and the Hanoi regime were ready to put their signatures to a peace document. Only South Vietnam still objected to the terms on the table, under which 150,000 N.V.A. troops would remain on South Vietnamese soil. Control of the country would effectively be split with Saigon ruling only those lands where it had sufficient military force to hold. Thieu voiced those objections one last time, saying the terms were *'tantamount to surrender'*. Nixon slapped him down yet one more time by threatening the end of all aid if Saigon didn't sign to the peace agreement.

On January 23rd 1973, President Nixon announced to the world that terms had been agreed that would *'end the war and bring peace with honour.'* Four days later the Peace Accords were signed in Paris by all parties. The war was finally over – at least as long as you didn't live in Vietnam. The Vietnamese regimes, both North and South, saw this merely as America going home. There would still be a mighty reckoning some day between North and South.

TIDYING UP

America's involvement with Vietnam started to unravel with almost indecent haste. On the day that the Peace Accords were signed, the U.S. Secretary of Defence Melvin Laird officially ended the draft. Mid February saw the first of 591 American prisoners of war returning home from North Vietnam under Operation Homecoming. Everyone who was coming home would be back by April 1st. The U.S. Navy even rather magnanimously helped the North Vietnamese to neutralize the mines

President Nguyen Van Thieu

ABOVE LEFT: President Nixon escorts Nguyen Van Thieu, to his car following a meeting | ABOVE RIGHT: A view of a downtown street in north Vietnam

clogging their harbours.

On June 19th 1973, Congress passed the Case-Church Amendment. This expressly forbade the United States from getting involved militarily in any future conflict in South East Asia as of August 1973.

THE CAMBODIAN MESS

Since the war was now over, as far as America was concerned, it was safe to start having recriminations, breast beatings and witch hunts. In July 1973, the U.S. Senate Armed Forces Committee began hearings into the secret bombing of Cambodia conducted by the U.S. during 1969 and 1970. The committee heard from Secretary of Defence James Schlesinger that no less than 3,500 bombing raids had been carried out against supposedly neutral Cambodia. These raids, he said, were launched to help prevent assaults on American troops by the N.V.A. who had no regard for Cambodia's neutrality and were using it both as a base of operations and a hiding place.

By August 14th, all U.S. strikes against Cambodia were stopped, in accordance with the Case – Church Amendment – and there were repeated calls for President Nixon to be impeached for his role in ordering and supporting the secret bombing.

To further limit the power of the president to wage war in any future conflict without the agreement of Congress, the War Powers Bill was passed on November 7th 1973. This required any future president to get assent from Congress within 90 days of sending U.S. troops oversees to fight. Nixon tried to use the presidential veto- but failed. The idea was clear. No more Vietnams. America had had a bellyful of foreign wars – and more.

FOR THOSE LEFT BEHIND

While America legislated and tidied up their mess, Hanoi had no time for such niceties. The ink was barely dry on the Peace Accords when, in March 1973, a high level meeting was held between top politicians and military commanders. The objective – to prepare for a major offensive against the South. Plans were made to build a massive new road into the Mekong Delta to ship supplies south, along with the construction of a 3,000 mile oil pipeline and improved radio communications.

In the field, there was constant fighting with total disregard for the Peace Accords literally from day one. By the end of the year, it was reported that 13,788 South Vietnamese troops had been killed in battle, along with just over 45,000 communist soldiers and over 2,000 South Vietnamese civilians. Furthermore, U.S. Intelligence reported that the N.V.A. had infiltrated 70,000 more soldiers into South Vietnam during the year, along with 400 tanks. They'd also built 12 new airstrips in the South.

America had effectively left Vietnam to its fate.

NEXT PAGES; TOP LEFT: NVA officer makes sure US POW's papers are in order | CENTRE LEFT: Recently released United States POWs await take off | BOTTOM LEFT: Wives at Camp Pendleton, California. Waiting for the Return of Prisoners of War | MAIN IMAGE: American servicemen, former prisoners of war, cheer as their aircraft takes off from an airfield near Hanoi as part of Operation Homecoming

ARVN Prisoner of War Repatriation. Prisoners of War shed their prison uniforms and shout political slogans following their arrival for repatriation

1974

Richard M. Nixon releasing the transcripts of the White House tapes

WATERGATE

In May 1974, Congress began proceedings to impeach President Nixon over the Watergate scandal. On August 9th, he resigned the presidency and Vice President Gerald Ford became the next president of the United States of America.

It's almost impossible to overemphasise how traumatic these events were to the American nation, how introverted and heartsick the nation became. Hardly anyone noticed when, in September, the U.S. Congress approved just a meagre $700 million to help the South Vietnamese. Hardly anyone in America that is, but in Saigon the message was all too clear. America had other things on its mind now and next to no interest in the fate of South Vietnam. $700 million impoverished the A.V.R.N. and the Saigon regime struggled to pay their troops' wages. Hanoi noted the reduced funding with interest too, and understood all too well what it meant.

PHUOC LONG

In October 1974, the powers that be met in Hanoi to discuss America's internal chaos and increasing estrangement from the cause of South Vietnam. They had also noted increasing unrest in the South and demonstrations in Saigon against President Thieu and what were claimed to be his repressive policies. The time looked right to tear up the Paris Peace Accords in their entirety and invade the South. The more aggressive members of the Hanoi Politburo wanted to lash out with a full scale attack as soon as possible. The more cautious among them wanted to check the American response first. When really pushed, it was conceivable that America might wake up and unleash its massive air power against Northern forces. The cooler heads prevailed. They would test the Americans first.

Special Agent George G. Liddy who was the Nixon Administration liaison and leader of the group of five men who broke into the headquarters of the Democratic National Committee at the Watergate Complex

Aerial view of Vietnam railway service repair crews clearing right of way and installing new track

On December 12th 1974, the N.V.A. unleashed their 4th Army Corps against A.R.V.N. troops in Phouc Long, part of Binh Phouc Province close to the Cambodian border. The area was especially significant because it contained the strategically important Route 14 highway. The A.R.V.N. units fought with determination and courage – but as they struggled to hold and were gradually overrun in some towns and bases, one thing soon became clear. There were no American jets in the skies raining down bombs, white phosphorous and Napalm.

The Americans really had gone home for good.

ABOVE: A cartoon from One of a variety of anti-Ford buttons generated during the 1976 presidential election | **RIGHT:** Followers of PANV in South Vietnam

Despite the ceasefire, the fighting continues in South Vietnam

1975

US President Gerald Ford

US Embassy, Saigon

POISED TO STRIKE

'The Peace Treaty was our death warrant'

President Thieu.

By January 6th 1975, the whole of Phouc Long Province was in North Vietnamese possession. Hanoi's test had been successful. They had well and truly broken the Paris Peace Accords and the worst they had received from America was some angry diplomatic communiques from the newly appointed President Ford. Nothing that mattered.

As Phouc Long fell, Hanoi was already preparing an outright invasion of the South. It now had the fifth largest army in the world – and the enthusiastic support of the Russians in particular, who were providing every sort of aid possible as they revelled in America's post-Watergate confusion and weakness. Hanoi planned to commit 22 Divisions to the invasion of the South and anticipated it would take some two years to achieve victory.

In the event, it would take just 55 days.

American analysts knew what was happening. In January 1975, President Ford warned Congress that the North had 290,000 troops in the South ready to lash out at the beleaguered Saigon regime, well supported by tanks and heavy artillery. Secretary of Defence James Schlesinger also warned that America was failing to live up to its promises to defend South Vietnam. Congress wasn't interested. When President Ford virtually begged them for $522 million in military aid for Saigon, they turned him down flat. Not only would America not send fighting

A Marine provides security as Sikorsky CH-53 helicopters land at the Defense Attaché Office compound

planes and ships to defend the South, it would not even provide money to support the South's own fighting forces.

On February 5th, General Dung secretly smuggled himself into South Vietnam to lead his N.V.A. troops to final victory.

THE MARCH OFFENSIVE

Dung launched his attack on March 10th 1975, with 25,000 troops attacking Ban Me Thuot in the Central Highlands. The City fell in just a day as over 2,000 of the 4,000 A.R.V.N. soldiers defending the City deserted it or else gave themselves up to the enemy. They understood that, without American support, fighting on was pointless. In Saigon, President Thieu took the decision not to try to defend the Central Highlands and two neighbouring provinces. He called a hasty retreat for the A.R.V.N. units in the area. As the N.V.A. forces swept in to take possession of the abandoned territory, before them streamed a vast and totally chaotic mass of soldiers and civilian refugees all desperately fleeing south. The exodus became known as the 'Convoy of Tears' – and the N.V.A. shelled it ruthlessly, ripping into fleeing soldiers and civilians indiscriminately.

Events took on a bloody momentum all of themselves. Dung accelerated his plans and struck the South harder and faster than he had ever planned. On March 19th, Quang Tri City fell and then Tam Ky five days later. A growing flood of panicked civilians and demoralised soldiers joined the human tide of refugees streaming south down Route 7B. The refugees and soldiers continued to be attacked brutally. Of the estimated 60,000 A.R.V.N. troops retreating South, only 20,000 ever reached their destination

South Vietnamese soldiers are forced south by North Vietnamese troops heading for Saigon

South Vietnamese refugees arrive on USS Hancock

on the coast. The others were simply overwhelmed in the retreat, stripping off their uniforms and hiding amongst the civilian population or dying in the frequent attacks.

A desperate President Thieu gave strict instructions that the city of Hue was to be held at all costs. It fell on March 25th after just a three day siege. The refugees fleeing before the victorious and utterly ruthless N.V.A. Army now numbered in the millions, many streaming towards what they thought was the relative safety of Da Nang. Instead, Da Nang proved to be a death trap. Civilians and soldiers died in droves as they fought to escape the doomed city via its airport, harbour and beaches before it too fell to the enemy on March 29th. A.R.V.N. officers deserted their own men, leaving them to find their own way out of the shattered and burning ruins of the city. Most simply surrendered. Whole fighting units simply ceased to exist.

Now America did intervene – helping to provide ships to rescue those trapped against the sea.

THE HO CHI MINH CAMPAIGN

The invasion had gone better than General Dung had ever dreamed of. Now he renamed his offensive the 'Ho Chi Minh Campaign' and received instructions from Hanoi to press on as hard as possible. They wanted to take Saigon before the end of April 1975 – and Dung was ready to try.

By 1st April, over half of South Vietnam was in the hands of the communists and the N.V.A. were swarming south. Only heroic resistance

Crewmen of the amphibious cargo ship USS Durham (LKA-114) take Vietnamese refugees aboard a small craft

ABOVE LEFT: USS Midway refueling USS Badger in the South China Sea, April 1975, during Operation Frequent Wind | **ABOVE RIGHT:** Air Force HH-53 Super Jolly Green Giant helicopters being refuelled on the flight deck of the aircraft carrier USS Midway at the beginning of "Operation Frequent Wind"

by A.R.V.N. forces of the 18th Army Division at the city of Xuan Loc, just 38 miles from Saigon, brought their seemingly unstoppable advance to a halt. The communists threw 40,000 men against the city. Still, it held for almost two weeks, and over 5,000 N.V.A. soldiers died fighting to seize it.

PRESIDENT THIEU RESIGNS

On April 20th, the American ambassador, Graham Martin, met with President Thieu and strongly recommended he resign. The next day, Thieu addressed his beleaguered nation for the very last time. With tears streaming down his cheeks, he bitterly read out Nixon's promise of help should Vietnam ever need it. South Vietnam had been betrayed, he declared, by the Paris Peace Accords, Henry Kissinger and America. '*The United States has not respected its promises,*' he said. '*It is inhumane. It is untrustworthy. It is irresponsible.*' Shortly after, the C.I.A were ushering him on a flight to Taiwan and into exile. His three tons of gold bullion were shipped separately.

SAIGON IN THE GUNSIGHTS

100,000 N.V.A. troops were now speeding south to Saigon, which was a city in utter chaos, filled with desperate, cowering refugees and the shattered remains of A.R.V.N. units, many having abandoned much of their fighting equipment on the road south. On April 27th, N.V.A. troops finally encircled the capital and began firing rockets into its heart. They were, General Dung said later, '*like a divine hammer held aloft*'. The city was

being softened up, its morale drained, its people terrorised. The next day, General Duong Van 'Big' Minh (one of the original conspirators in the coup that saw President Diem killed) was appointed as South Vietnam's last president and appealed to the North for a ceasefire.

He was ignored.

WHITE CHRISTMAS

At noon on April 29th 1975, the American Service Radio in Saigon played 'White Christmas' by Bing Crosby. It was a coded signal. To those in the know it meant only one thing – 'Get out now!' President Ford had initiated Operation Frequent Wind – a helicopter evacuation of the city. Forty U.S. Navy ships including three aircraft carriers now lay 200 miles off the coast ready to receive the evacuees, who would be choppered out to the fleet on board giant CH-53 Sea Knight helicopters. Each evacuation wave would take an hour out to the fleet and an hour back after refuelling.

Originally, the main point of escape for American civilians, embassy personnel and valuable Vietnamese was the air base at Tan Son Nhut but that had been bombed and shelled out of action. The evacuation was moved to the grounds of the American Embassy instead. Despite the best efforts of Marines in full combat gear, the Embassy was soon in danger of being overrun by ordinary Vietnamese desperate to escape the doomed city. The first choppers arrived late, exacerbating the tension. Those in possession of the correct papers were guided into helicopters and whisked away. Those who didn't – some 140,000 middle and lower rank

ABOVE LEFT: More South Vietnamese refugees seek the safety of the US Navy | **ABOVE CENTRE:** South Vietnamese UH-1H is pushed overboard to make room for a Cessna O-1 | **ABOVE RIGHT:** Another South Vietnamese helicopter is pushed over the side of the USS Okinawa

Vietnamese employees – were abandoned to their fate.

Joining the refugee fleet were choppers flown by South Vietnamese pilots, carrying their own friends and family. As these touched down, they were emptied and then the chopper unceremoniously slung over the side of the carriers to make room for the next inbound refugee flight. It all looked like desperate chaos. It was. It was also the largest helicopter evacuation in history, pulling 1,000 Americans and 6,000 South Vietnamese from the doomed city.

The last Americans – Marine guards from the embassy – were out by 8.35am on April 30th. At 11am, a single N.V.A. tank crashed through the gates of the Presidential Palace. The world's media missed it and so the communists dutifully re-enacted it for their cameras. Shortly after, the flag of the Viet Cong flew over the Presidential Palace and President Minh agreed to unconditional surrender. Accepting the South's surrender on behalf of Hanoi, Colonel Bui Tin told Minh,

'You have nothing to fear. Between Vietnamese there are no victors and no vanquished. Only the Americans have been beaten. If you are patriots, consider this a moment of joy. The war for our country is over'.

In the aftermath of the fall of Saigon, there was no bloodbath and no mass executions. 200,000 South Vietnamese officials and bureaucrats were sent to re-education camps and citizens of Saigon judged to be too bourgeois for their own good were packed off to new homes working the paddy fields in the countryside.

Bing Crosby, 'White Christmas' singer

North Vietnamese troops take the presidential palace

North Vietnamese troops in front of Presidential Palace gate

POSTSCRIPT

2.8 million American troops served in Vietnam. 58,000 died. A further 300,000 were wounded, of whom 30,000 were totally disabled. The high percentage of wounded and seriously injured compared to the dead was down to the excellent Medevac flights and field hospital units America deployed in Vietnam. More of those who would have died of their wounds lived and came home, maimed but alive. But there are wounds and then there are wounds. In the mid-1980s, it was officially estimated that almost 2/3rds of all Vietnam veterans were in need of psychiatric counselling. At the start of the 1980s, almost a quarter of all G.I.s who had seen 'significant combat' had been arrested for criminal offences, often drug or violence related. Humiliated by a messy and unwinnable war, America largely shunned its veterans. They were an embarrassing reminder and when it was time for 'Johnny to come marching home again', no parades were organised. Today, America has the mightiest arms – but in Vietnam, it discovered it had an Achilles heel - the very freedom that it was fighting for and the virtues for which it stood.

Over two million Vietnamese are thought to have died in the conflict.